CW00953660

Prison Time in Sana'a

Prison Time in Sana'a

By Abdulkader Al-Guneid

Introduction by Dr Stephen Day

Copyright © Abdulkader Al-Guneid

ISBN: 978-0-9929808-7-0

Published in 2021
By Arabian Publishing Ltd
50a High Street, Cowes, Isle of Wight, PO31 7RR, UK

Arabian Publishing Ltd is an imprint of Medina Publishing Ltd

Medinapublishing.com

Cover Designed by Jem Butcher
Edited by Nick Cash

A catalogue record for this book is available from the
British Library.

Printed and bound in Great Britain by Clays Ltd, Elcograf S.p.A.

Contents

Map of Yemen

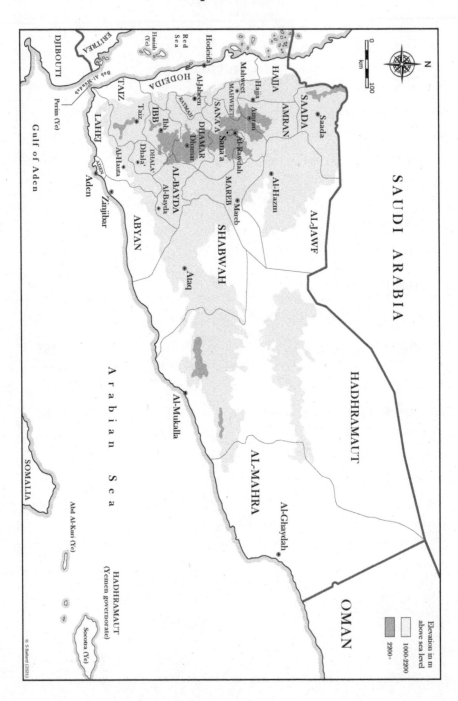

Map of Taiz, Yemen

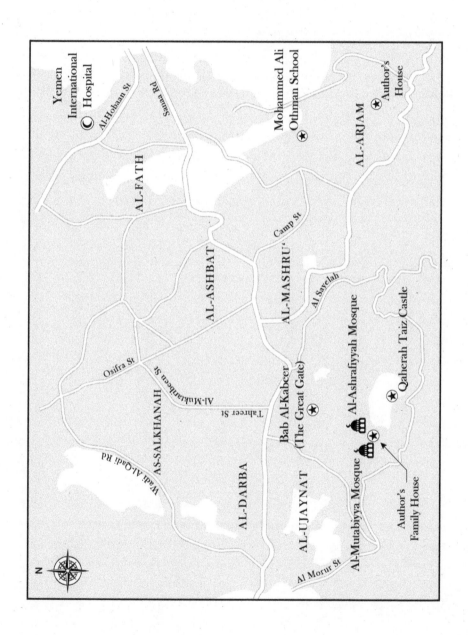

Introduction

In 2011, when Yemen adopted the 'Arab Spring' model of street protests from Tunisia and Egypt, Dr Abdulkader Al-Guneid was among the country's best-known social media commentators in Arabic and English. His hometown of Taiz, where he worked as a well-respected physician, witnessed the first youthful calls for the downfall of the regime in early February. This occurred at a downtown location named after the celebrated protest square in Cairo, Maidan al-Tahreer, or 'Freedom Square'. The protests spread quickly to Sana'a and other Yemeni cities. During 2011 and the years that followed, Dr Al-Guneid reported regularly on Facebook and Twitter until his kidnapping and disappearance in August 2015.

The ancient Romans labelled Yemen 'Arabia Felix'. But the Arab Spring did not lead to a happy outcome. Instead, Yemen witnessed economic mismanagement and collapse between 2012 and 2014 before a coup overthrew the transitional government in January 2015. Two months later, international warfare erupted as Saudi Arabia and the United Arab Emirates led a coalition of states that attacked to prevent the forces behind the coup from seizing control of the entire country. Over the past six years, both Britain and the United States have played key arms support and supply roles in the coalition that has waged a highly destructive military campaign against the Houthi militia, which continued to enjoy support from Iran with shipments of sophisticated weaponry backed by logistical, financial and technical assistance.

Years ago, the United Nations began to refer to Yemen as "the world's worst humanitarian crisis". This occurred after the spread of famine and disease added to the misery of the war's death toll. Today,

Yemen continues to hold this ignoble title as it confronts the Covid-19 pandemic.

****

During the early phase of Yemen's protests in the spring of 2011, I reconnected with Dr Al-Guneid after looking for news of Yemen on Twitter. I first met the physician and visited his home in Taiz during the mid-1990s, when I lived for two years in the country while conducting research for a PhD dissertation on the politics of Yemeni national unification. This research later became the basis of my book, *Regionalism and Rebellion in Yemen: A Troubled National Union* (Cambridge University Press, 2012).

In 2011, following my reconnection with Dr Al-Guneid via Twitter, it was unsurprising to learn that he served as an international source of informed opinion on events in Yemen. News sources around the world, including the BBC and The New York Times, regularly sought interviews with him after discovering his social media posts. I knew Dr Al-Guneid as a reliable source of information on Yemeni politics during my doctoral research the previous decade. We first met one year after he led a grass-roots peace movement in Taiz that attempted to prevent a brief civil war in the spring of 1994. This was a few years after the historic unification of North Yemen and South Yemen in May 1990.

Prior to unification, Dr Al-Guneid served as mayor of Taiz in the 1980s. In early 1994 he and some associates circulated a petition that received 100,000 signatures from people urging northern and southern politicians to maintain peace and preserve national unity. The quest for signatures failed in its ultimate purpose of preventing warfare, but it gained nationwide attention at a time when the hopes and dreams of millions grew following elections in 1993. These were the first free and open elections ever held on the Arabian Peninsula. In a sense, Dr Al-Guneid's drive symbolised the democratic aspirations of the country. Unfortunately, the space for democracy closed after 1994.

During the years immediately after the 2011 protests, which Dr Al-

Guneid and many others considered a new opportunity for democracy to extend its roots in Yemen, I regularly encouraged him to compile some of his social media posts into a collection for publication as a political memoir. I saw other social media commentators publish such books, yet he always replied, "If you want to go back through my Twitter account, then feel free to write the book yourself".

Once armed forces loyal to former president Ali Abdullah Saleh allied with Houthi rebels from the north in Saada governorate to overthrow the transitional government in a coup, before marching south from Sana'a to Taiz and Aden in February and March 2015, I warned Dr Al-Guneid of the risks if he continued to post his opposition views on social media. I feared he would be targeted by Saleh or the Houthis. But he was defiant, vowing to continue reporting how the country's democratic spirit endured.

When Houthi militia kidnapped Dr Al-Guneid from his home in the summer of 2015, I was deeply concerned for his safety. I joined others who drew attention to his disappearance and demanded the help of governments around the world to obtain his release. Prison Time in Sana'a is his account of his time in captivity.

****

Following the author's release from prison in 2016, we spoke by telephone once he reached Canada to begin life in exile with family. I said: "Now you have the basis for your memoir". He did not then express any intention to write this book, preferring instead to withhold the fact that he was already drafting its chapters. About a year later he sent me an email announcing, "I did it; the manuscript is finished". In order to judge my reaction, he sent three chapters for review. I was enthusiastic, telling him that he had a gem of great value on his hands.

I like to think I played a part in helping to achieve the book's potential, but my role was minimal. It was an honour to serve as primary editor of the early long manuscript, which Dr Al-Guneid wrote entirely on a mobile phone, as he was accustomed to doing whenever he posted text on social media back in Taiz. I offered advice whenever I could. He was often uncertain how the book would be received, and he frequently became despondent that it would never appear in print. I played an important role by lending encouragement to inspire him to remain optimistic and add more details about Yemen's rich history and culture.

I told Dr Al-Guneid that, for me, as a person fond of America's best literature by the great author of Mississippi River fame, Mark Twain, the tales he told of life inside the walls of a Yemeni prison – a prison built with funding from a US counterterrorism programme to hold Al-Qaeda inmates – compared favourably to the best tales Twain ever told of life along the big muddy river's shores. I also said his work fitted in the tradition of the best Arabic and Persian literature, extending back to the tales of *djinn* and magic carpets that the great Harun Al-Rashid heard told of Scheherazade. As a work of literature, *Prison Time in Sana'a* fits somewhere between the two because Dr Al-Guneid is a master storyteller.

He is one of a handful of Yemenis today who have sufficient knowledge of the country's history to explain its complex politics and culture. It is one of the most fascinating lands in the world, where traditional Arabic poetry is still preserved as a living artifact in tribal *zamel* (poetry). Most Yemenis hold millennia-old religious views of predestination, and many still believe superstitiously in *djinn* and magical incantations. This is true of characters throughout Dr Al-Guneid's story, nearly all of whom were inmates of Yemen's National Security prison who shared the same dark, airless cells with the author. They and their inventiveness, creativity, deceits and raw humour could come from the pages of any Twain novel.

****

Readers will instantly appreciate the value of this well-written book. With wit and wisdom, Dr Al-Guneid manages to explain the social structure of a country divided along multiple lines with tribal and non-tribal populations. He discusses the different fighting prowess of tribes that live in Yemen's broad desert versus those in its spectacularly high mountains. He explains the background of Hashemite *sayyid* who claim descent from the family of the Prophet Mohammed and now support the rise of Iranian-style Shia politics under the party of Ansarallah, which is modelled on the Hezbollah in Lebanon.

Yemen's Hashemite *sayyid* historically allied with mountain tribes to rule a millennium-long series of Zaydi dynasties. Dr Al-Guneid also describes various Sunni religious trends including the Muslim Brotherhood, Salafis and supporters of Al-Qaeda, many of whom were resident in the same prison. Cellmates relied upon one Al-Qaeda inmate to decipher the meaning of their dreams, which they withheld from the guards by secretly communicating through an ingenious system using the building's plumbing.

Dr Al-Guneid's role as a physician trained in scientific methods is an important part of *Prison Time in Sana'a* because, during his imprisonment, he was called upon by administrators to diagnose and treat the ailments of inmates, serving as unofficial prison doctor. The juxtaposition between the author's trust in science and the superstitions of individuals around him shapes the book's narrative. This includes the story of an American Baptist who was arrested at Sana'a airport after trying to enter the country to complete work on a residence facility used by US Embassy staff. The Baptist's religious outlook mirrored that of most Muslim inmates, including those with Al-Qaeda. The author describes a revealing exchange between the American and members of that group during a visit to the prison's outdoor yard.

A main theme of the book is the daily struggle to maintain hope and sanity in order to survive depressing circumstances in prison. Dr Al-Guneid describes the heart-wrenching story of sick inmates left untreated when the medicine he prescribed was not supplied by prison officials. Like so many individuals disappeared and held captive around the world, the author recounts how he spent his days concerned less about his own well-being than that of family, his wife and children, especially his youngest son, Mustafa.

More than a physician, the author is a civics educator who, like Plato and Aristotle, engages in discourse about the social and economic well-being of the wider population. This is greatly needed at a time when the country has collapsed and its politics descended into factional power struggles that betrayed the nation. Dr Al-Guneid is well positioned to lead the discourse as a former adviser to both the governor of Taiz, Shawki Ahmed Ha'el Sa'eed, and the city's street-fighting resistance leader, Hamoud Al-Mikhlafi. All Yemenis will recognise in Dr Al-Guneid's memoir the abiding love for and trust in their homeland that is necessary to restore what makes a uniquely good life for all of its people.

****

Prison Time in Sana'a is in three parts. Part One is a personal account of Dr Al-Guneid's time in prison as remembered from his new home in Canada. Part Two offers further commentary about the political background to conflicts in Yemen arising from the 2011 Arab Spring. Readers unfamiliar with events in Yemen may benefit by reading sections of this part as they proceed through Part One. Part Three contains a brief afterword by the author reflecting on the days following his release from prison and his current life in exile.

I would like to thank Medina Publishing, its founding director Peter Harrigan and staff for bringing this memoir to publication, providing readers the pleasure of discovering Dr Al-Guneid's talent as a storyteller, while deepening their awareness and understanding of Yemen's current plight. In-house editor Nick Cash deserves special credit for helping to condense the text to a length suitable for publication. Special thanks are due to Dr Saud Al-Sarhan for his support along the way.

Stephen W. Day

PART 1: PRISON DIARIES

Chapter 1

The gunmen came for me at 3:00 in the afternoon. When they drove me away an hour later, I didn't know if I would ever see my home again.

It was 5 August 2015, and I was being abducted from the home my wife Salwa and I had built together – the home where we had celebrated my 66th birthday just three days previously.

Before this, it had been as ordinary a day as it could be in a city at war. Months earlier, Houthi militia and Republican Guards loyal to ex-president Ali Abdullah Saleh had overrun my hometown of Taiz, and as a consequence the city was constantly being hit by airstrikes from the Saudi-led military coalition fighting against the takeover.

That fateful day I had, as usual, risen before dawn, done my usual chores, followed the news, posted on social media and phoned whomever I thought would know what was happening on the ground. This included people living locally inside and outside my city. I loved to survey the temperament of the silent majority, whether in urban neighbourhoods or in the countryside.

Deep in my heart I felt that I represented the silent majority – the heart and soul of any society. They work hard, produce, reproduce and make any place tick. They are the taxpayers to the state and they pay the price for its mistakes.

By 1:00, I had finished following every bullet, gun shell and air strike across my beloved city. Afterwards, I felt I should do something physical to rid my system of emotional tension. So, I started exercising on the multilevel patio of our home. I ran, sprinted, climbed and carried weights before enjoying a swim in the pool under the early-afternoon sun.

During all of this activity, I was regularly interrupted by local phone calls. I also responded to international calls from foreign broadcasting stations enquiring about what was happening in Taiz. They knew about me from my presence on social media.

After my exercise routine, I paused for lunch. I never have breakfast, taking only bitter coffee, tea and water during the whole morning, and the meal tasted so good. On Thursdays and Fridays, we usually eat traditional Yemeni food with meat and consommé. Since the beginning of the war, however, we ate much less in quantity and quality, partly because of the imposed siege and partly because we had to economise.

For a long time, we lived on our savings. I was forced to sell some of our properties to cover daily expenses. Over the past decade, all professionals had seen their incomes and purchasing power diminished. We all started to live on savings and asset sales. There is no longer a middle class in Yemen.

In mid-afternoon I was watching the news on television when things changed abruptly as Salwa shouted that a Houthi militia vehicle had just stormed into our yard, blocking the main gate behind it. I got to my feet and rushed to the window to see with my own eyes what was happening. There was a pickup truck full of armed and uniformed men wearing armbands with the slogan (*sarkhah*) 'God is great, death to America, death to Israel, curse on the Jews, victory to Islam' – a trademark of Houthis.

From a window on the second floor, I shouted to their leader: "What are you doing on my land? Get out! May God take your soul from your chest!" (This is a typical Yemeni way of saying 'get lost'.)

He responded by gesticulating with his Kalashnikov, ordering me to come down.

I was in shorts, so I quickly put on a pair of jeans and posted on Twitter and Facebook that armed Houthis were at my door. Usually, I would post both in Arabic and in English for my foreign followers – but this time I only had time to post a quick message in my own tongue.

Descending to the ground floor, I found five armed men in the main hall. It was immediately clear that they were Houthi sympathisers from Mount Sabr, the 3,000-metre peak that overlooks the city. They were a faction of whom most sensible citizens were ashamed because of the harm they had been causing since the uprising.

In response to my repeated demand that they get out of my home, the leader – the biggest of them – brusquely ordered me to go with them.

"I'm going nowhere with you," I answered defiantly – but he seized me roughly, twisting my arm behind my back, and dragged me barefoot into the courtyard.

I realised that there was no use resisting so, instead of letting anger overwhelm me, I forced myself to stay calm. I wanted to absorb every moment as it occurred without any distortion of fear or anger. Quietly and calmly, I asked the Houthi ringleader – whose name I knew to be Akram – for some footwear. He refused, continuing to twist my arm as he forced me to the main gate.

"Okay. Let go of me. I'll go with you on my own," I said.

Once again, he refused, hauling me to their pickup and shoving me in the back seat, where I was squashed between two of his henchmen. Another sat in the front while the rest of them remained inside my house.

I continued to try to remain calm, not wanting to give them the satisfaction of seeing that I was worried. Instead, I mocked the gunman on the front seat, saying to him: "Now, can you do the Houthi *sarkhah* for me?"

Immediately and theatrically he did so, waving his clenched fist in the air, cursing America and Israel. I was amused. I just couldn't believe that a rational person would do this so proudly and on demand. How could this be happening inside my usually sensible city?

From the truck I could see Akram sitting on the steps leading from my terrace. One of his compatriots emerged from inside the house clutching my Galaxy mobile phone and Salwa's two iPhones. Akram shouted to me, asking if they were mine.

"That one is mine. The others are my wife's. Give them back to her," I demanded.

He shook his head vigorously – a big 'no'. I said nothing. This silence, as I found on so many later occasions, was the most eloquent answer to my captors whenever they denied my requests.

Changing the subject, I asked him his full name.

"Akram Abdulghani Al-Guneid."

I didn't like that we shared part of our names, even though my family has no relationship to the Al-Guneids of Al-Sarari of Mount Sabr – who think of themselves as Hashemite *sayyids*. This was a group that had welcomed the Houthi takeover of Yemen, believing they had a divine right to dominate, being descendants of the Prophet Mohammed (Peace Be Upon Him).

These people and others like them have long since been nicknamed locally the 'Friday *sayyids*', the joke being that anyone born on a Friday is a *sayyid*, or master. It is a way of belittling their claim that they are special compared with the *sayyids* from the northern part of the country between Sana'a and Saudi Arabia.

The Mount Sabr *sayyids* are a Sufi sect who would chant on religious occasions and perform as quack doctors, writing spells to invoke or chase away genies – referred to as *djinn* in the Arab world. Because of their claim to be *sayyids*, Houthi leaders had contacted them, calling them 'cousins' who shared a noble bloodline. The Houthis made similar seductive overtures to factions throughout Yemen. Few could resist the temptation of being considered more noble than other groups.

Previously, Taizi *sayyids* had never claimed a divine right to rule Yemen, nor had they served among the governing imams. They had not provoked conflict or killed their countrymen to assert supremacy – actions that had been all too common among northern Yemeni *sayyids*.

Now, however, they were giving free licence to Houthis from Saada to come to our region, which is why most residents of Taiz felt that they were betraying their own people. They provided men on the ground who were willing to kill their own people. They gave fake legitimacy to the Houthis by means of their local support.

My own Al-Guneid family were landowners from Thi Al-Sufal in the neighbouring governorate of Ibb, who had long served in the judiciary and in government. By contrast, my abductor, Akram Abdulghani Al-Guneid from the nearby neighbourhood of Al-Gahmaliyah, was well known for extorting money from local market traders and street vendors, beating up those who refused to pay. Few refused.

People like Akram had been used by President Saleh's supporters ever since the outbreak of Yemen's political turmoil in February 2011. Street bullies and ex-convicts were sent to attack opposition street demonstrations. Saleh even opened jails in order to allow prisoners to swell the ranks of the rabble, serving as instruments of the Republican Guards and the Houthi militia. This proved highly effective, disguising wholesale political intimidation as minor local disputes. It was a tactic I was now experiencing at first hand.

Akram came out to the truck, having allowed Salwa to send out a pair of flip-flops for me. He sat in the front, next to his brother, and boasted to his compatriots guarding me that they had found compromising items in my house.

"Is he ISIS?" they asked.

He replied that I wasn't, drawing that conclusion from the piano, paintings and statues inside, all of which would be considered *haram* (forbidden) by fundamentalists. They asked instead if he had found Saudi currency – could I be a Saudi agent?

"No, this one could even pay the Saudis," he said, gesturing at my three-storey villa, pool and grounds.

Houthis liked to see themselves as agents of God sent forth to carry out his will. Whoever stood against them was either ISIS or a traitor bought by the Saudis. On this occasion, Akram offered another explanation: "This one wants to be a hero. He wants to be another Che Guevara. A socialist!"

I was amused by this exchange and, while it was absurd, what attracted my attention most was the intimacy between the men.

After a while, more of them emerged from my house and squeezed themselves into the back of the truck. The gate was opened and I was driven away.

As we left my home behind us, Akram smirked at me as he looked at the looted smartphones, saying: "Facebook is aflame for you".

Over the years, I had become a well-known social media commentator about what Saleh and the Houthis had been doing to my country, because of my ability to post quickly in both Arabic and English. This was why I was now being driven away to an unknown fate.

I asked myself whether I should be afraid – and surprised myself that I was not.

The car took the asphalt road through the hills to the foot of Mount Sabr, where Akram taunted me that I was being taken to the mountain peak where I would be in danger of Saudi air strikes. It had been reported on the local news that the Houthi rebels would place their abductees in places likely to be hit by coalition air raids, simultaneously getting rid of opponents and smearing the coalition.

In fact, he had just been trying to scare me. We drew up to a government broadcasting site, where I was locked up after being warned not to try to escape and mocked about the danger that I was in from air strikes. I was left alone in a large *magyal* (a room used for qat gatherings) with huge windows looking north over the city, east to Mount Sabr and west to Al-Qahirah castle. Two hours later, Akram and his men returned, saying "Sheikh Hamoud Al-Mikhlafi rang your phone".

At the time, the sheikh was commander of the People's Resistance, a title I had popularised in my social media posts. My abductor was his sworn enemy.

"What did he say?" I asked.

"I didn't answer him," replied Akram.

I was then given a coat to put on over the thin white T-shirt I wore – even though it was August, Taiz could be cold in the late afternoon – taken back to the truck and driven in the direction of my home.

For a moment I thought that I would be returned and this nightmare would soon be over, but we sped past the road leading to my hillside neighbourhood of Al-Humaira and a sadness swept over me as it receded behind us.

To occupy myself as the truck sped along, I began to formulate some rules of thumb for my forthcoming captivity, promising myself that I would be a source of pride not only to my family, friends and all those who were with me in the same trenches, but also to my country. I was determined that I wouldn't show any sadness or regret. I would not collapse. I would not show if I was hurt. I would not ask for anything. I would silently endure any hardship, hunger, pain or need. I would overcome any yearning for my family. I would keep my spirits high and my mind and intellect sharp and intact.

I would exercise as much as I could to help me stay quiet, calm and collected. I would use my ability to contemplate and dream, sailing to worlds far away. I would be stoical. I would ask for nothing, but if anything was offered, I wouldn't say no. Self-preservation and resilience are good. Stubbornness is not.

****

It was dark by the time we arrived in Houban Valley. The two Abdulghani brothers were in the front seats. I was squeezed between two armed men in the middle row of seats, with three more armed guards in the back.

Akram handed my phone to the guard on my right and asked him to see if I had been in contact with anyone in Saudi Arabia. He found nothing. Then Akram asked him to see if Ahmad Al-Mosawa's phone number was in my contacts.

Al-Mosawa was one of the Houthi political leaders in Taiz, though originally from Udain in Ibb governorate. He had been a judge, but in recent times had given up this respectable occupation to devote himself to the Houthi cause, travelling regularly to the Houthi stronghold of Saada to receive his instructions.

He once told me that their supreme leader, Abdulmalek Al-Houthi himself, was aware of me on account of a review of a book about the Houthi movement that I had published in America. He also told me that Al-Houthi liked my writings about Al-Qaeda, in which I described it as a movement that had been conceived, nurtured and raised in Yemen, and then used, abused and misused for the purposes of Saleh, other regional powers and the US.

I had often invited Al-Mosawa to my regular social gatherings to sit together with people from all political parties to discuss matters in a cordial atmosphere. At the time, I believed that all parties and cliques, especially those in Taiz, squabbled with each other for no particular reason and that sitting together might warm relations and help avoid conflict.

At this point Akram's phone rang. He listened, continually saying: "*Na'am, sayyidi*" (Yes, Master), adopting a northern accent and assuring his 'master' that he had set all of the right surprise traps for those who might attack that night.

My heart was heavy as I listened to the sounds of war all around us. Each night I would hear explosions and shell-fire, but that night I was especially wary of what Akram's conversation could mean.

Before we reached Taiz airport, the truck stopped beside another vehicle, and I was ordered out. Armed men handcuffed and blindfolded me before pushing me into the other car. I was then driven away by this second group – whose accents clearly showed they were from the north.

Chapter 2

After a short drive, I was taken from the car and led – still handcuffed and blindfolded – into a building. I was made to stand facing a wall. And then my interrogation began. It would continue for five exhausting hours.

Two men questioned me. By their accents, one was from Taiz and the other was from the north. I asked which branch of the security forces they were from, and the northerner claimed they were merely 'God's supporters', saying: "You want to make a hero of yourself – who do you think you are, Che Guevara?"

That was the second time I'd heard Che mentioned in just a few hours. I would really have liked to know what their fixation with him was.

They still had my phone and Salwa's and were now going through my emails.

"Not bad," said one. "You're an intellectual. But how could an intellectual like you not support us? You must hold regional prejudices, but how can you be an intellectual and regionalist at the same time?"

I didn't bother to respond. I could hear that they were chewing qat and smoking a hookah – and seemed to have reached *bihshama*, a qat-induced state of mild euphoria.

They were also clearly enjoying having the upper hand over me, sounding off and making wisecracks as I stood there, bound and blindfolded. Nevertheless, I wasn't rattled and, despite their prattle and the suffocating tobacco-laden air, I tried to remain calm. Only a few times did I respond, quietly and coldly. At other times I mocked them and told them off.

I was asked if I supported the Saudi attacks and, when I denied it, was told my phone showed them otherwise.

"No one likes to see foreign aircraft attack his own country, but Saudi airstrikes don't concern me right now," I said. "What does concern me is your guns and rockets hitting my neighbourhood! What concerns me is your snipers terrorising my sisters in their own houses! What concerns me is that most of my family has been displaced from our own homes! What concerns me is that my youngest son couldn't sit his exams, and that I had to send him to Canada for his safety!"

They did not reply.

The Taizi kept searching my phone and was now trawling through my WhatsApp account. He wanted to know the identities of those in the resistance, and the name of the medics who had been sending me pictures of people injured in the conflict.

I didn't help them, saying, "The names are with you already – what else do you want from me?"

Then he came across my correspondence with resistance leader Sheikh Hamoud Al-Mikhlafi. He thought he'd struck gold and launched a barrage of questions. It was futile to deny our connection – and anyway I cannot lie.

"Why run in circles?" I said. "Yes, I'm with the resistance. Yes, I want Al-Mikhlafi to defeat you."

A momentary silence fell; I don't think they expected that response.

Instead, the northerner asked me if I knew about a recent popular demonstration in which, he claimed, the people had given the Houthis a mandate to govern.

"We are the state," he said. "You say you are with the resistance and we say you're guilty of high treason, and you should be tried for it."

This was frightening. I knew that the punishment for high treason was death.

Next, they questioned me about what weapons I had in my house. "None," I replied truthfully. "I don't even know how to load a gun."

"That may be so, but your words are stronger than bullets."

I took this as a compliment and smiled inwardly. It was important to feel victorious based on reason and logic, giving the right answers at the right time.

In Taiz, unlike areas of the north, we rely upon skill and intelligence. Taizis prosper when there is a well-functioning state capable of enforcing the rule of law. All prosperous kingdoms throughout Yemeni history arose from the people of Taiz and neighbouring communities with a similar culture.

By midnight, their questions had ceased and my handcuffs were removed. Still blindfolded, I was told to apply my fingerprint to interrogation papers that I could not see, but I didn't bother to object. And then I was left alone.

Soon I was led along a corridor and up some steps into an apartment, where my handcuffs and blindfold were removed. My guard had a Kalashnikov over his shoulder and a torch in his hand. I glimpsed a bathroom, two closed doors and a worn mattress on the floor before he left me in darkness, locking the door behind him.

The next morning I awoke early. From the bathroom window, I could see where I was being held – near Taiz airport in a suburb dubbed 'Saleh City'. Incessant shell-fire resounded as Saleh's army bombarded the city.

I was brought a breakfast of beans, bread and tea – the first food I had eaten since my abduction. After eating, I spent my time exercising. From time to time I would look out of the bathroom window, from where I could see what looked to be northern tribesmen dressed in *thobes* and jackets with daggers tucked in their belts and Kalashnikovs slung over their shoulders.

Later that afternoon I was brought a meal of chicken, vegetables, bread and rice in takeaway bags from a local restaurant. It wasn't bad, but I ate little of it. A pleasant surprise came later when they brought me qat – a real treat.

Outside, the shell-fire continued, and the time passed slowly. So regular was the noise that I managed to ignore it and imagine it was silent, at least until darkness fell and a huge explosion shook the building.

I knew immediately it was a Saudi missile – which, despite the danger to me, pleased me greatly. As I would do were I at home, I rushed to the window to see where it had hit, just as another explosion followed. With the building shaking even more, I thought it best to move away from the window, so groped my way in the dark to my mattress and sheltered in the corner, where I hoped I would be more protected.

A third strike not only shook the building but also shattered windows along the corridor. A fourth did the same on the other side of the building. Then silence, with neither artillery nor air strikes. Had it been four planes, or one launching four missiles? It didn't matter. What mattered was my pleasure.

I didn't think I was alone in appreciating these coalition attacks on Houthi and Saleh positions. Rather, I believed that millions of Yemenis welcomed them, and were downhearted when there were no Saudi aircraft in the sky.

An hour later, a grim-faced soldier opened the door. He wore a khaki uniform and carried a Kalashnikov. He looked younger than 20 and seemed both sad and scared.

He ordered me to my feet and, after refusing my request to use the toilet, rushed me out of the building to a small van parked near the main entrance to Saleh City, where he handed me over to two armed tribesmen.

It was 9:00 as they sped me away, driving recklessly along the dark, sinuous roads. I could see house lights twinkling on the slopes of Mount Sabr, some 20km ahead of us. A wave of despondency fell over me as I longed for my home up the hillside. Perhaps, just perhaps, they would let me return to my family, I thought.

But it wasn't to be. A short while later we rendezvoused with a larger, dirtier truck manned by six qat-chewing militiamen who, by their accents, were from Saada, 500km north towards the Saudi border. They bundled me inside and we set off into the night.

The driver drove with his foot pressed hard to the floor, but the vehicle was underpowered for the terrain, so on every incline he would ride the clutch. Soon I could smell burning rubber.

As we drove north, memories of my childhood came to me, including a verse my mother would repeat in my bedtime stories when the hero was fleeing an evil spirit: "Land appeared ahead, and land behind we left without end. And all lands praise the only single God of the universe."

But I wasn't fleeing from a *djinn* – I was being abducted by one.

I didn't know where I was being taken, but some time later we came to a tarmac road and I concluded that we must have climbed Al-Nagd Al-Ahmar mountain on the way through Ibb governorate, a thought that made me lose all hope of returning home.

As we continued through the night, the men passed a bag of tobacco amongst them, adding a pinch to the mass of qat already in their mouths. They hardly needed the extra stimulant, but it did confirm to me that they were from the Houthi heartland of Saada, where the people are known for their fondness of this mixture.

The moon was full as we drove on, my captors periodically shouting the *sarkhah* or *zamel*, a northern tribal chant. They were warriors returning home triumphant after capturing their enemy – in this case, a 66-year-old doctor from Taiz who had never borne arms in his life.

After passing through the city of Ibb, I reconciled myself with the bitter fact that they were taking me to Sana'a, where I thought I would be an offering to their clerics and leaders – and consequently in grave danger. Nevertheless, even knowing into what danger my actions had led me, I also knew that I would do exactly the same again. After all, if someone like me didn't raise their voice, who would?

We continued driving dangerously fast northwards over the uneven roads, pitted from years of underfunding during the later years of Saleh's regime as well as from bombing by coalition aircraft. However, the driver seemed to anticipate every obstacle. He was also able to negotiate our smooth passage through the frequent security checkpoints. These were manned by a rag-tag selection of guards dressed in a variety of threadbare uniforms or shabby tribal clothing with daggers in their belts and nothing more than rubber flip-flops on their feet – a common sight at road checkpoints, in ports, at tax offices and elsewhere throughout the country.

Sadly, this was the case not only during the present war but more generally too, even in times of peace. Many highway tolls were in fact operated as private fiefdoms by officials who had bribed their superiors to be appointed to such profitable posts. Of course, it was ordinary citizens who suffered.

At each checkpoint, our driver would mention the name 'Abu A'del' and the barrier would immediately be removed. I surmised that this was a password that was probably changed each day, but at one checkpoint a hapless guard didn't seem to know the drill and went off to find his boss to see what he should do. My guards became impatient and the driver disembarked to speed things along. One of his compatriots, gesticulating and spraying tobacco and qat, urged the driver to ignore the guards and drive on.

"Just tell them that we're armed!"

Our driver got back behind the wheel and we drove off, leaving the checkpoint guards staring at us open-mouthed.

By contrast, at a checkpoint in the plains after the Sumara mountain pass, the password was met with great respect. Our driver took the opportunity of siphoning fuel from a stash of drums, paying with a thick wad of banknotes. Petrol and diesel were not often available at gas stations, the militia controlling the black market for fuel and selling it at exorbitant prices. Indeed, a large proportion of their income came from withholding vital commodities; although their leaders blamed the high prices on the war, in truth they were profiteers.

It was past midnight as we drove through the mountains. The temperature dropped and I began to shiver from the breeze coming through the broken window beside me. Despite this my exhaustion laid heavy on my eyelids and I drifted into a fitful doze, constantly woken by bouts of shivering, which made me feel even worse. With all my might I tried to stay awake and overcome my discomfort.

Finally, we arrived in Sana'a, but the driver, who had appeared to know every pothole on the road from Taiz, didn't know his way through the streets of the capital, and was constantly on his phone for directions to the National Security headquarters in Shou'oub. From this I surmised he wasn't employed by the government. I also learned that he was to deliver me to someone named Mohammad Al-Sharafi.

Chapter 3

It was before dawn when we pulled up in front of the National Security HQ near the famous Bab Al-Yemen gate. Mohammad Al-Sharafi was waiting for us.

The driver had clearly been in charge during the trip, but when he jumped out of the van, he became subservient. The contrast between the now-meek, emaciated driver and the tall, broad Al-Sharafi was marked. The latter was a *sayyid*, and our driver was now reduced to a simple tribesman, craning his neck to look up to his superior.

Instead of worrying about my safety, I became preoccupied with this scene. I was well aware of traditional relations between sayyids and tribespeople in the history of Yemen's northernmost mountains, and was enjoying watching it play out, both men seeming to be acting their roles for my benefit.

On social media, many commentators described these roles as 'Qandeel and Zenbeel', meaning the candle and the straw basket (leaders and blind followers), nicknames that poked fun at both the *sayyid* and the tribesmen. (I had my own nicknames for these two groups: *madaleez* (crazies) and **malahees** (zombies).) Bringing my enjoyment of this charade to an abrupt end, 'Qandeel' plucked a set of handcuffs from his pocket and manacled me roughly, at which point 'Zanbeel' turned his gaze to me – the first time he had paid any attention to me since we had left Taiz.

It seemed the whole world was watching and wanted to know what I felt. I continued to retain my dignity and detachment, but I saw myself as one who was in the right but had fallen into the hands of evil forces. I truly believed that was how the watching world would have judged the situation. I was also looking forward to a happy ending.

Al-Sharafi searched my pockets, demanding my identity card. I explained that I didn't have it with me, having been kidnapped from my own home with no chance to bring anything.

"Yes, you were innocently doing nothing. They just took you like this, for no reason," he mocked. Then, rather more threateningly, he growled: "You are ISIS".

I couldn't contain myself and laughed: "Not that again!"

He reappraised me scornfully, drawing out every syllable: "Mog-aaaaaa-wameh" (Resistance).

I smiled to myself grimly as Al-Sharafi blindfolded me and bundled me inside the building. Now I had become one of the 'forcibly disappeared', vanishing into the Houthi-occupied capital.

I was manhandled along a high-ceilinged, cold corridor, which I could occasionally glimpse below my blindfold. It was expensively tiled, carpeted in the middle and with luxurious wooden doorways leading off it –an Ottoman-era building, I concluded, very possibly one of those refurbished for Turkish president Erdogan's recent visit to Sana'a.

Before I was given a space on the floor to sleep, I asked to use the bathroom, and Al-Sharifi grudgingly released one hand from the cuffs, led me to the facilities and warned me not to "do anything heroic". I was then ordered down onto the red carpet and told to sleep, having been refused a blanket. Despite the chill, I felt the tension seep from my tired body and was quickly overcome with sleep.

Shortly afterwards, though, I was awoken by someone having difficulty breathing and I realised I wasn't alone. Someone moved towards the struggling man and was rudely ordered back to his spot.

"I have to help him," a voice replied. "He's my brother. He's sick and just had an operation on his chest in Jordan."

Soon, however, the man's tortured breathing eased, and he seemed to fall asleep – as did I.

When I next awoke, I could see the morning light coming from the end of the corridor. It was eerily quiet.

"Is there anyone around?" I called out. "I need the bathroom."

There had been a change of guards and a new one led me to the end of the corridor and unshackled my right wrist. I went inside and undid the blindfold. From the window, I caught a glimpse of the top of one of the city's characteristic old buildings, confirming that I really was in the 200-year-old building that had been taken over by the security services and used first by Saleh and later by the Houthis as an interrogation and internment centre.

I put my blindfold back on and came out, but I could still make out a masked and khaki-clad soldier with a Kalashnikov on his shoulder. He replaced my handcuffs, tightened the blindfold and then led me back to my place, where I was ordered to lie down.

A considerable time later, I was given a small breakfast of bread and beans, which I ate hastily while still bound and blindfolded. It was the first food I had eaten in almost 24 hours. Around me, I could glimpse several other prisoners. We were not allowed to sit, stand or speak, being instructed to "lie down and keep your mouths shut".

Later came a simple lunch of rice, potatoes and a small piece of meat. I ate with reluctance. The silence was total and, due to the blindfold and my ordeal the previous night, I dozed intermittently until the evening – which was when my interrogation began.

Darkness had descended and it was quiet and still when I heard heavy footsteps along the corridor, the buzz of voices and the banging of doors.

By now there were more people sitting along the corridor. I remained handcuffed on the carpet in the middle, peeking from behind the blindfold. I could hear people being questioned beyond the closed doors.

Soon, I was ordered to my feet and taken into one of the rooms. Glancing from under my blindfold I could see three men sitting Yemeni-style on a carpet-covered mattress, their arms resting on rectangular bolsters. Their leader was dressed in a pressed white *thobe*, over which he wore a tailored dark waistcoat. He turned his head aside as I entered the room, wary that I might be able to see his face.

I was ordered to sit on a battered sofa, from where I could make out someone on a chair in front of me dressed in a *ma'awaz* – similar to a long Scottish kilt. From his accent I could tell he was from my home region.

Sitting next to the leader was the one asking the questions, though he clearly wasn't the one directing the interrogation. In the middle of some questions, he would suddenly halt and then ask something out of context. Whenever he stopped in the middle of a sentence, it was as if someone was signalling him not to proceed or not to press me so hard. The real bosses were in the background, unseen and unspeaking.

To begin with, the questions were about me and my family, and my position in the community. I told them truthfully that I had been elected mayor of Taiz Municipal Council in 1980, that I had led a large grass-roots anti-war movement in 1994 and that Saleh himself thought of me as a dissident. I was asked if I knew who had arrested me.

"Houthis," I replied. "They were wearing the *sarkhah*."

I was then asked if I had been arrested before and replied that I had been imprisoned by President Saleh for a few days in 1995, a year after the civil war, as punishment for my anti-war activities.

"Heh! You have a record ...," my interrogator commented triumphantly, halting in mid-sentence. I deduced that his boss had signalled him to stop what he was getting at.

Instead, I was asked what I had done to annoy the Houthis, as if those in the room were not involved in my kidnapping.

"I did nothing. So many other people did much more than I did. There could easily be a million people like me on social media. What's wrong with expressing one's opinion? Anyway, before the coup, I didn't strongly oppose either side. I even think Houthis were pleased with what I wrote for RAND in America."

I was referring to an extensive analysis I had contributed to the well-known US research organisation concerning the origin of the Houthis, which I knew even Abdulmalek Al-Houthi himself had read.

"Americans! Did you say Americans?" he exclaimed, ordering one of his companions to write that down. Apparently, a written record of my questioning was being compiled.

When the interrogator unexpectedly changed the subject, I once again understood the boss must have signalled him to drop his attitude and that this was all some game of cat-and-mouse.

"When did you begin your opposition to the Houthis?"

"When Al-Ghouli carried his Kalashnikov and shouted 'Peace' as he besieged Amran," I replied, referring to 'Sheikh' Al-Ghouli, who caused Saleh loyalists and Houthi militia to flock towards Amran and Sana'a, encircling both cities. This was clearly an expensive exercise and was suspected to have been financed by Saudi Arabia and the UAE.

The interrogator seemed ready to grab me by the throat but was restrained by his boss, who seemed to appreciate my answers. Everyone in Yemen had laughed at the so-called 'Sheikh' Al-Ghouli, who bragged of bringing change to Amran by peaceful (*silmiyah*) means, while he prepared to besiege the city armed to the teeth.

"But what in particular did you write that upset the Houthis?" the interrogator asked.

I was beginning to enjoy the line of questioning. In general, I liked the idea that they believed in the power of my writing.

"No idea. I can't tell why they're annoyed with me."

"Okay, tell us what was the last thing you wrote," he demanded.

"About a nightmare ... a very long nightmare," I said.

He was incredulous. "You say 'nightmare' and you don't expect them to be angry?"

"For God's sake, with all of these things happening in Yemen, don't you find it a nightmare?"

Again, he changed tack. "Do you support the Saudi aggression?"

The words poured from my mouth. "I know that there are tanks in the streets of Taiz shelling our neighbourhoods. With my own eyes I have seen howitzers targeting residential areas from the presidential palace and I have seen the smoke from Katyusha rockets hitting people's homes. They are shelling civilians indiscriminately. I know of snipers killing innocent passers-by and shooting into bedrooms across the old city. I know that members of my family have been forced from their homes. I know that you have totally lost our support in Taiz."

The interrogator remained silent. It was over. For the second time, I was made to put my fingerprints on papers while blindfolded and handcuffed without knowing what was written on them.

I was asked if I had any requests, replying that I resented being bound and blindfolded and having to ask permission to use the bathroom. I asked if they had my phone and Salwa's.

The interrogator said he didn't know if the phones were sent from Taiz or not, and I was led back to my place on the red carpet and ordered to lie down on the floor. I did not – I sat.

****

One of the armed soldiers in the corridor asked where I was from. When I told him, he asked how things were there.

"People are being shelled in their own homes and snipers are shooting innocent passers-by," I replied.

"What about you? What did you do?" he continued without any intent of interrogation.

"They say I don't like Houthi."

"We don't like Houthi either," he answered with a northern tribal accent.

I enjoyed the fact that he and other tribal soldiers did not admire the Houthis, despite the fact that Saleh's troops and the Houthis were working together to arrest people like me, incriminate us and put us in jail.

Soldiers such as this man were from tribes from all around Sana'a. They were the embodiment of President Saleh's policy across four decades of militarising the tribes. He exploited national resources, state authority, government posts and military ranks in order to create a fusion of Sana'a's tribes into a military junta. People from the rest of the country – the south, the midlands, the east, the west and the far north – were largely excluded from positions of power. Saleh's own family and the Sanhan tribe formed the nucleus of his power, while the Sana'a tribes acted as a shield, which he used to tighten his grip on the country as he prepared to pass control to his eldest son, Ahmad, his intended successor.

"Are you with the Saudi attack and aggression?" the soldier asked me, encouraging me to speak frankly.

My spirits were high after my interrogation, and naively I replied at some length.

I explained how I believed that we Yemenis had failed badly in two ways: in not building a good relationship between the people and the government, and in not improving people's living conditions. Consequently, tension had spread all over the country, causing a bitter struggle between the regime and the rest of the country, with a cycle of conflict and face-offs that no one could win. With each phase, the country worsened and the social fabric was further torn as extremist ideologies became mainstream. From a failing state, the country had become a full-blown failed state.

I went on to explain that, because of its strategic location at the entrance to the Red Sea and proximity to the world's richest oilfields, regional and global powers thought they would lose too much if Yemen collapsed.

Pausing to see if he was still paying attention, I continued, telling him at length what I thought about all the events that had led to the Saleh-Houthi coup, the role of Iran, the intervention by the UN and neighbouring countries, and the attempt to agree a new constitution. But after the coup, the Saudis had felt in danger of being surrounded by Iran and its allies, which is why they launched military operations.

"When they intervened, most Yemenis were pleased – us in Taiz in particular," I said. "We didn't support the coup in Sana'a, so of course protests flared up when Houthi troops arrived. That's why we approve of Saudi Arabia's intervention."

After I had finished, he asked coldly: "And now, who will win?"

"War needs money," I replied.

"Al-Za'eem will find a way," he said, referring to Saleh. "He'll crush them all."

After Saleh had been forced to resign, he didn't like being referred to as 'the deposed president', so he nicknamed himself 'Al-Za'eem' (the Chief). His followers used this as a term of affection, while the rest of the country used it to mock him.

It suddenly became clear that the soldier didn't agree with any of my arguments. He was sure Saleh would eventually prevail. In his estimation, Saleh would conquer the lands between Taiz and Aden, then destroy the Houthis, and lastly defeat the Saudis. Eventually he would close his fist on all of Yemen and start a family dynasty.

As I finished my conversation with the soldier, someone brought beans and bread, which I ate while still handcuffed and blindfolded.

Gradually, the sounds of movement and talking subsided, and as silence returned I fell asleep; but I was soon awakened by the same coughs and gasps that had disturbed me the night before.

This time I tried to diagnose the sufferer's problems. I believed it was wasn't asthma, a heart problem or a neuromuscular problem and was unlikely to be a case of malingering. Rather, I concluded, it might be a case of hysteria convergence. The man's brother seemed good at what he did to ease the man's suffering. Wondering if I too could help him, I at last managed to doze off again as the morning light appeared through the window at the end of the corridor.

Chapter 4

I t was still early morning when I woke. It was quiet and everyone else was still sleeping, but soon I heard footsteps coming along the corridor. I was taken to the bathroom – with my cuffs still on – and brought back to my place, where a guard was ordering us to be silent and setting rules for bathroom breaks.

I needed to stretch my body, so got to my feet and made myself as comfortable as I could, but I was then kicked in the back of one knee for the amusement of one of the laughing guards, who was mocking my hometown.

"How honourable for your tribe," I muttered. "Since the beginning of history, this situation between a captive and his guard has been acted out. A man's honour is proven by how he acts in times like these. I guess it's up to you to choose where to put your name."

The guard fell silent – and stopped kicking me.

Nevertheless, I was full of bitterness at my treatment, and declined breakfast when it was brought, deciding that I would refuse to ask for anything from my guards, even to go to the toilet. I had a half-empty water bottle from the day before and moistened my mouth with little sips throughout the day.

Later that morning, the main guard led me and my fellow prisoners, still blindfolded and handcuffed, to a small room, and crammed us onto a small sofa from where he could continue to question us. Dressed in a white *thobe* and jacket with a traditional dagger in his belt, he stopped in front of me. Amid a lecture on patriotism, he accused me of being a traitor and a Saudi agent, wondering how I, an educated man, could fail to understand the things he did. He was a perfect example of those in Sana'a who had enjoyed exercising power for over three decades of former President Saleh's rule.

What struck me most was the man's hypocrisy. I had never been on a Saudi bankroll, but he most likely had, coming from a tribal population whose sheikhs had been supported by Saudi Arabia for decades. During my entire life, I never heard of Saudi financial payouts to prominent people in Taiz. We never ate or drank except by the sweat of our own labour. It was the powerful tribal sheikhs of Sana'a and lands north of the capital who were Saudi agents.

When lunch arrived, I refused again. The same bitter taste lingered in my mouth, making it impossible to accept food. It seemed that the chief guard's way of talking was having an effect on me. I knew of bitter experiences and bitter situations, but I had never realised they could manifest as an actual bitter taste in the mouth.

Later, when someone asked whether I was on hunger strike, I said no, I was just feeling nauseous. Early on, I had indeed considered the idea but quickly rejected it. I was determined to keep myself in good health and spirits. A hunger strike would never be on my agenda, at the top of which was self-preservation.

When darkness fell, the guards took us back to the corridor to lie down. The evening meal of bread and beans arrived, yet the bitter taste remained in my mouth and I still refused to eat. Time passed slowly as my thoughts meandered. Thoughts of loved ones brought a lump to my throat. I felt sad not for myself but for them, wondering what effect my abduction was having on them.

Someone bent down beside me and whispered: "What did they accuse you of?"

"They say I don't like Houthi," I answered.

"I don't like Houthi either. But what did you do?"

"I posted on Twitter and Facebook about what was happening in Taiz, about the shelling and snipers, and how the ordinary people are suffering."

"Those Houthis are dogs," he replied, "but don't worry – if it was only Twitter and Facebook, I will get you out."

His accent was northern and he sounded self-assured – possibly one of their leaders. But soon he was gone. It was always easy to distinguish between Houthis and Saleh loyalists, not that it made much difference to me. I just liked to make an assessment. Houthis clearly worked together with Saleh's supporters, but they hated each other. Each was waiting for the day to get rid of the other.

****

From the moment I was kidnapped, I kept trying to determine who was the ultimate villain behind my ordeal: Saleh or Houthi? Was I a victim of one, or of a combination of both? I had once written on social media that the Houthis were the handkerchief on which Saleh blew his nose.

Even the so-called 'Six Saada Wars' between Saleh and the Houthis were part of Saleh's intricate 'snake dance', a term that came from an interview in which Saleh once memorably claimed that ruling Yemen was like "dancing on the heads of snakes".

My musings were interrupted when a gang of soldiers rushed in and ordered us all to our feet. Our blindfolds were tightened and it soon became clear we were being transferred. I was led out of the corridor and down several flights of stairs before being bundled aboard a crowded van, ordered not to move or talk and driven quickly away.

Chapter 5

A short, hair-raising drive later, we screeched to a halt. The driver sounded the horn and I could hear a gate open. The van drove up a ramp and passed through a second gate before coming to a stop, when we were ordered out of the van and led along a corridor into a reception room, where we were told to remove our blindfolds.

I was being transferred to the main National Security jail – a place that would be my 'home' for the next 300 days, not that I knew that at the time. The location of the prison was meant to be top secret, but I was later to learn that it was in Saref, on the eastern outskirts of the capital. It was a big, modern, concrete-and-stone edifice, built with US money to house Al-Qaeda prisoners. Dug into a rocky hillside, its exterior was shielded by various administrative buildings and a military camp. Nearby was a UN compound and a community college.

At last, I could see people clearly, though just by the light of a battery torch, as there seemed to be a power cut. Nevertheless, I enjoyed using my eyes again, at the same time wondering how I could find pleasure in anything while surrounded by such hateful creatures, horrible conditions and tragic events.

While a guard removed my handcuffs, I held onto my blindfold, saying that I would like to keep it as a souvenir.

"Yeah, and we will give you golden handcuffs as a souvenir, too," muttered my jailer.

The ones I was wearing certainly weren't precious metal – but they were a sturdily built, British-made model, of a type that the UK exports all over the world. I later joked with a British friend that he should be "very proud" of their quality.

I could see that we were a group of eight lined up against a wall. For the first time I felt that I was in this ordeal with others, rather than completely alone. But who were they? Surely they couldn't be accused of the same things as me?

Item by item, the jailers took whatever we had. I had nothing except the plastic flip-flops on my feet and a toothbrush. As my flip-flops were taken, another jailer snatched my toothbrush from my hand, but I was eventually permitted to keep it. The only light came from a single torch as our names were recorded and our belongings bagged up.

I was standing next to a huge, unfriendly-looking man. "*Salam alaikum*," I said to him, but he turned his back on me. I felt very uncomfortable.

The jailers brought seven mattresses and eight blankets, there being insufficient floor-space for all of us. Fortunately, two of our number were related and happy to share a mattress. One corner of our cell was taken up by an ablutions area, separated by a hip-high wall. Even with just seven mattresses in the room, there wasn't much chance of any privacy when using these basic facilities.

With a stony face, our jailer warned us to behave and, locking the door behind him, he left us in total darkness. One by one, we made our way toward the wash corner, where there was a plastic cup and a bucket under a tap – and a simple hole in the floor. These basic sanitation arrangements were to become all too familiar in all the cells I was to stay in.

Eight prisoners packed like sardines in a tin container without adequate space, light or air. Everyone wrapped himself in his blanket and said nothing.

"Does anyone know roughly what time it is?" I asked to break the silence.

"Shut up and sleep," the large man replied. I didn't react, and soon started to doze off.

Just as I had been in National Security headquarters, I was woken by my cellmate's breathing difficulty. The same two prisoners instantly jumped to his aid. They banged on the cell door and asked for some air and a torch. A jailer gave them one and left the small inspection hatch in the door open.

In the gloom I could see the man hyperventilating. To me it looked like a psychological reaction. His peers could understand illness but were less likely to be sympathetic to what could be seen as weakness, so his unconscious mind mimicked symptoms to mask his distress. Luckily, his relatives were able to calm him, whispering familiar Bedouin endearments.

We all watched as they fanned him. One told us about their uncle's lung problem, but he didn't like it at all when I offered my diagnosis. As the distressed man calmed down, soothed by the familiar words, we were all able to wrap ourselves in our blankets and sleep.

I woke up before daylight to the sound of dogs barking. Hummingbirds fluttered nearby, and the giant snored loudly beside me. My gaze drifted to a faint light on the top of the wall, where a plastic pipe opened. It was the only source of light and air from outside – but also, unfortunately, of insects. However, it was the first daylight I had seen for several days, so I enjoyed watching the play of light and shadow across the cell's wall, projecting images of faces and animals in constantly shifting patterns.

The hatch in the cell door was unlocked, and our breakfast was thrust through – the usual beans, unleavened bread and tea. It was my first food in 36 hours, yet I still wasn't hungry.

****

Among my cellmates were the Al-Hadda brothers – the elder of whom suffered the breathing problem – and their nephew from Hareeb in Shabwah governorate. They had been arrested for smuggling gold across the border. Then there was the 60-year-old owner of a currency exchange business, together with his son-in-law and nephew, who both worked for him. Originally from Duba'a in Taiz governorate, they had settled in Sana'a and had not returned home for 30 years. The seventh was the taciturn giant, Balsan, the security guard at their currency bureau, a native of the capital's old town, albeit with proud tribal origins.

All had been arrested when Houthi militia interrupted a transaction, seizing 170 million rials (more than USD 500,000 at the time). Mansour Al-Haddad, one of the gold merchants, said that troops had suddenly appeared, grabbing the money from the Houthis and dispersing them. All my cellmates were then arrested and sent to National Security headquarters, where they were accused of being Saudi spies and using proceeds from the gold to fund the resistance. Clearly, not even the interrogators took this claim seriously, but it was an effective way of extorting funds from merchants. Al-Haddad assumed that, after the security bosses had taken a cut, he would get some of his capital back and all seven of them would be released.

The money-changer's son-in-law wanted to know why I – a respectable doctor – had been arrested. When I told him about my blogs, he advised me to simply write something flattering and our captors would let me go.

"Not if it was the last day in my life," I said.

Both the gold merchant and his nephew were called Mansour. The younger of the two quietly quizzed me: "Doctor, you had a comfortable life. What made you antagonise them and bring all this hardship down on yourself?"

"So, people like you don't one day ask me what I did when these people were destroying our country," I explained.

He was not convinced. Indeed, I wasn't always sure myself. Many times, I would ask myself why I put myself and my family at risk in this way. I used to say: "It's either a proud head raised high on an erect neck, or I don't want them". If people like me stayed silent, who would speak out? What would I say to my grandsons when they asked what I did during the war?

Balsan wanted to know whether we Taizis took sides with the Saudis against Yemen, threatening, "I swear by God we will burn you alive and destroy your homes one by one".

I was simmering with rage, which I expressed later that afternoon when he insulted me and my hometown once more.

"Behave yourself and keep your mouth shut! Not another word about me or Taiz, or else."

His boss, the currency exchanger, quickly intervened, while the elder Mansour proclaimed that we were all brothers going through the same ordeal, so we should help each other instead of fighting. The heat went out of the situation, but I was secretly pleased with the outcome of my outburst.

Mansour senior gazed at the ceiling and said to no one in particular that what they had taken from him was the sweat and hard work of his entire life. He would never give up what was his right, no matter what. Then he started to pray, beseeching the Almighty for help. His words flowed eloquently, but soon his breathing sped away from him and he suffered another attack, at which his brother leant into his chest, while the younger Mansour fanned him. Each time he recalled his predicament, he would become so distressed that his conscious mind could no longer bear it, and his symptoms returned. Whenever this happened, his brother and nephew would gently tend to him and ease his anxiety.

On our second night in that overcrowded cell, the door was flung open and two of us were told to get out. Since the others were related, this would be Balsan and me. The two of us were going to get to know each other a lot better, as we were to be put together in a cramped single chamber.

A simple doorman, Balsan ordinarily would not have been included in the arrest, but, thanks to his big mouth, he got himself arrested alongside his employers.

As soon as we'd been locked in our new cell, Balsan laid his mattress out, taking up most of the floor-space, wrapped himself in his blanket and fell fast asleep. I got as comfortable as I could and concentrated on controlling my emotions.

I imagined Balsan as a patient in my clinic in Taiz, making a quick diagnosis of his snoring. Like the rest of him, Balsan's neck was fat. I imagined looking at a CT scan showing layers of fat around his laryngeal aperture, which right now was the source of a deep snore on every single inhalation. So closely was I wrapped up in my study of his snores that I soon dozed off to sleep.

When I awoke, it was just after dawn. I really needed to wash. After seven days of not washing or changing, I was disgusting even myself. Fortunately, there was a little detergent powder in the latrine area, so I soaped myself down and washed my underwear. Of course, I didn't have a towel, so I put my jeans on without underwear and reluctantly put on my dirty white T-shirt. I then prayed.

At around 9:00, the sounds of breakfast finally woke Balsan, who leapt to his feet and grabbed our rations through the hatch. He quickly returned to the floor and we began gobbling down our bread and beans. As soon as he finished eating, he lay down again, covered his head with the blanket and started to snore once more. In our previous cell, Balsan had confided that he never had any trouble sleeping and could do so all day long. I was now seeing at first hand that he had not been exaggerating.

Later that day, having been woken for a paltry lunch, my cellmate asked me – in a much more conciliatory manner – why we Taizis were on the side of the Saudi aggressors. I tried to explain to him in a friendly way what I believed had brought our country to its current position. Yemen had been in dire straits before 2011, but at least there had been an agreed political process with the help of the UN and the Gulf Cooperation Council (GCC). As I began explaining the impact of the armed coup launched by the Houthis and Saleh in 2014, I heard Baslan snoring again. That was my cue to stop preaching.

****

Balsan talked loudly with a domineering, nasal tone that he used to overpower those he was addressing. He was proud of his tribal lineage, saying that, if his tribe heard of his arrest, they would come fully armed to demand his release. But he also liked to embellish and exaggerate, claiming once to have been in the Military Police. I asked him why he had left, if that was so.

"You don't understand life, Doctor," he replied. "You don't know that they are all thieves, from the president right down to the lowest ranks. I couldn't continue unless I paid them."

At other times, Balsan claimed to have a degree in accounting, explaining he hadn't been able to pursue that career because of Saleh, who he thought was a habitual troublemaker. Despite this, and his apparent dislike of Houthis, he was willing to cheer on the destruction of Taiz.

The next day, Balsan asked me for a children's tale. He had previously heard me retell one of the stories my mother had told me as a child, in order to cheer up Mansour junior. Now Balsan was hoping I would be able to raise his spirits.

I point-blank refused. Not that I minded telling stories – it was just a case of establishing the pecking order. I could not stand a bully anywhere at any time, whether the bullying was directed at me or someone else. And I was determined to show Balsan that I wouldn't be bullied.

Later that night, Balsan awoke and asked me to fill him a cup of water. This huge man asked me, who was so much older, to serve him with water. In a firm tone that he couldn't fail to understand, I refused.

He backed down apologetically. A new order had been established. Soon, he was begging to be taken to another cell.

"This doctor is a politician who wants to brainwash me," he claimed. "I'm a poor man with children. Get me out! Take me to my friends!"

I shook with laughter. The man had gone from bully to child to being scared of me in the space of just a few hours. But later that night the jailers answered his prayers, taking me to my third cell. I never heard of Balsan again.

Chapter 6

The jailer opened the door to another cell to reveal my two new bearded cellmates. They were both eager to know why the door had been opened.

"Oh dear! God only knows what lies ahead for me," I muttered to myself – at which my jailer, taking pity on me as he locked me in, said: "Don't worry, they're alright".

The younger of the two men helped me with my mattress as his compatriot, Jamal, bombarded me with questions: my name, my hometown, what had I been arrested for and so on. He soon decided that I was a God-sent gift and was pleased that I had joined them in their dim cell.

Jamal was a sheikh of the Iyal Yazid Bani Suraih tribe from Amran governorate, north of Sana'a. He had been arrested because he was the only local leader who did not submit to the Houthis. He had been in detention since March, forcing his wife and daughters to fend for themselves for the previous six months.

"I was tortured for thirteen days," Jamal told me. "They burnt me with cigarettes, injected me with drugs and electrocuted me. Another time they put a shawl under my armpits while one guard pulled in one direction and another pulled my feet in the opposite direction, kicking me and dragging me up and down a stairwell, all the while blindfolded and handcuffed."

He had been taken to the National Security jail in Saref on the day Saudi Arabia launched its air strikes. He considered this as the first day of his arrest, ignoring the previous 13 days of torture he had suffered. His movements around the cell were proof of the damage that had been inflicted on him. He crawled awkwardly to the latrine and could only support himself with great difficulty while he relieved himself.

When he learned that I was a doctor, he wanted my opinion on his injuries, though I put him off until the morning as it was late and I was weary.

The following day, I examined his hands and arms. The small muscles of his left hand were wasted and his left arm was thinner than his right. I held his left arm, raised it and then let go. It dropped like a log until I caught it. He had no grip in his left hand. He could not even flex or extend his left wrist, elbow or shoulder.

As I examined him, he whispered: "Something I didn't say yesterday is that, three days after they pulled and dragged me up and down the stairs, a Houthi interrogator put his index finger in my groin and pressed down. It was so painful that I passed out and ten days later I found that I had only one testicle … I've never said this to anyone; you're the first to know. It's so embarrassing. I don't know why I'm revealing this to you."

He sobbed as he told me his tale, and I felt a lump form in my throat as I listened. I considered what must have happened. The interrogator would have found the spermatic cord and then pressed this against the pubic bone until the spermatic artery was occluded long enough to cause infarction of the testicle.

In short, Jamal had been castrated, but I did not tell him my diagnosis. Instead, I performed the same clinical examination on his lower limbs. I found that he had a similar paralysis below the waist; both his left limbs, upper and lower, were paralysed. This was the first case of flaccid hemiplegia that I had diagnosed since graduating from medical school in 1972.

These symptoms were most unusual; I couldn't think of a disease that would cause them. Dragging him up and down a stairwell must have injured nerves in his neck, while beating his buttocks injured nerves in his lower back. It was strange for an accident to affect the nerves on just one side. There was only one explanation: it was caused by torture.

"Regarding the paralysed side …" I began.

"I'm paralysed! I'm paralysed!" he immediately shouted in anguish.

Jamal had been paralysed for five months and hadn't realised. Instead, he thought he had a fractured bone that could be fixed. I wanted to explain how to preserve the muscles on his injured side and strengthen the muscles on his right, so he could maintain mobility. But after seeing his reaction to news of his paralysis, I decided to leave it for another time. He had heard enough for the time being.

****

Days followed nights and nights followed days with little interruption inside the dim, humid, suffocating cell. The only connection with the outside world was the small hatch in the door through which we were handed the same food at the same times, day after day, month after month: beans, bread and tea.

The person I most associated with the door hatch was Abu Sami, a giant guard who had to bend down to see through the opening, unlike his compatriots who had to stand on tiptoe. Abu Sami didn't like being disturbed during his night duty. At the start of each shift, he warned us not to create problems, yelling pre-emptive threats through the hatch. His mouth was always full of qat so he couldn't close his lips properly. We could always see the semi-chewed leaves there, even when he wasn't opening his mouth to yell at us.

Sometimes he would abruptly open the hatch after midnight, startling us as he peered inside by torchlight. I said to myself that when I was released, I would ask an artist to paint a picture of people cowering inside a dark cell as a horrifying face loomed through a door hatch. I envisioned a composite of Edvard Munch's 'The Scream' and Vincent van Gogh's 'The Potato Eaters'.

There were other times when the hatch opened long after midnight as National Security officials came to check on us. During the day, however, the hatch opening was something to look forward to because it usually meant mealtime, which most inmates eagerly awaited, plates in hand.

They would also try to exchange pleasantries with the cooks, some of whom were friendly and sympathetic, others less so. If one of us could glean a little information from the outside world in this way, he was considered a genius. Prisoners would always ask for more food to be put on their plates, which some of the cooks would do if there was enough. Guards sometimes accompanied the cooks, trying to catch out any inmate who started a conversation. They could be as aggressive with the cooks as they were to us; doling out food was meant to be done in silence.

****

I typically slept very little, so I had plenty of time to think. The hardest thing for me was thinking about my youngest son, 14-year-old Mustafa, who was in Canada. His school in Taiz had been closed since being occupied by Houthi troops. It was later damaged by Saudi air strikes because it was near the Republican Palace. You could see both the school and the palace from our house.

In the spring of 2015, Mustafa was preparing to sit his Grade 9 exams. My daughter Nagwan, who lives in Canada, realised that his visa from a previous visit was still valid and insisted that he go to stay with her. She isn't the sort of person to take 'no' for an answer.

When Nagwan was Mustafa's age, she was given a maple leaf pin by a visiting Canadian doctor who I had invited for a traditional lunch at our house. My daughter became fascinated by a country that had a leaf as its national symbol. She had always wanted to go to university in North America or Europe, and when she completed secondary school with flying colours, she came to me and said: "Baba, I will tell you a secret, but don't tell Mama".

"Okay," I replied.

"I told Mama that I wanted to visit Grandma in Sana'a tomorrow, but really I'm going there to sit a scholarship exam so I can study abroad. I've been emailing for months about scholarships to study in Canada."

I admired her spirit and gave her a kiss, although I knew Salwa wanted her to join her sister, Wigdan, who was studying architecture in Jordan.

Three months after sitting the exam and completing an online test, Nagwan was invited to an interview. I assured her that the panel already knew that she was clever and hard-working because of her school grades and exam results and that the interview would be about assessing her character. I prepared her as best I could with a series of mock interviews, which, to my delight, included similar questions to her actual interview. She was the only candidate to be accepted on the spot.

"Who am I to stop the dreams of such a girl?" I said to my sisters when they expressed their misgivings. Similarly, Salwa didn't like the idea of Nagwan leaving for Canada, but she eventually agreed.

After sailing through her studies at the University of Calgary, finding a job and enrolling in a master's programme, she eventually qualified for Canadian citizenship. For the past two months she had also been looking after her younger brother.

In my dim jail cell, I recalled driving him to the bus station. I had asked my handyman, Abdullah, to accompany Mustafa to Sana'a, where his brothers would take over and see him onto his flight. It was a complicated trip with many risks, especially for such a young boy. I remembered kissing him goodbye and driving away, pausing at a nearby roundabout where I could look back at him. He sat on the pavement waiting for his departure. I waved and he waved back. Neither of us smiled or showed any emotion, but I felt a lump in my throat, wondering if I would ever see him again.

Now, sitting under a blanket in jail, my eyes filled with tears as I wondered whether he was listening to his teachers and how often he thought about his family and country. I had to learn to suppress thinking about Mustafa because it was too painful.

Chapter 7

One gets the most essential information in jail from the old hands. In my case, this was Jamal. We shared a cell for three months, with a changing list of other cellmates. There was Shareef from Saada, who was released after a month, Sultan from Marib, who was moved to another cell, Mu'ataz from Syria, who was also released, and Abu Bara'a, another Syrian.

Realising that I was desperate for news about my hometown, Jamal assured me he would find out for me.

"What do you mean?" I asked.

"Through the water pipes," he answered.

"I don't understand."

"Wait and you'll see," he smiled, explaining that the pipes had to be empty. When our jailers were slow to refill the cistern, it would be news time. He explained that one could communicate only with neighbouring cells and those directly above or below. News had a way of spreading throughout the jail.

"But how do other prisoners know the news?" I asked.

"Some are near the guardroom and can hear them talking or listen to radio broadcasts. Or they hear from newcomers, as we did with you."

In our cell, we had a single tap in the small washing corner. There was a 10-litre bucket with water for our ablutions and a smaller one containing drinking water. We were careful to keep both buckets full at all times and routinely checked the pipes for news.

When the prison's water tanks ran dry, the big news day had arrived. Shareef squatted beneath the tap, sucked out the last dregs and, to my surprise, began speaking through the pipes as if using a telephone.

We were careful not to let the jailers know about our grapevine. It was always done discreetly, in a hushed voice. If we thought anyone was in the corridor, we stopped immediately. News was in greatest demand after any big explosion nearby. Often, inmates couldn't wait for the cisterns to run dry, so they would help them along, winding cloth around the tap to allow the water to drain silently into the latrine hole.

As well as for news, the "pipe network" was used to interpret dreams. For many, this was a primary concern. For example, dreams of being in Makkah were considered a good omen, portending release from jail. The ultimate authority on dreams was Tareq Al-Ma'eili, an Al-Qaeda leader from Marib. Jamal would listen to Tareq interpreting dreams for inmates in other cells, waiting for his turn to come. Handicapped with paralysis, he would crawl into the corner and contort his body to get his ear to the tap.

"Don't you want Tareq to interpret a dream for you?" Jamal often asked me. I always politely declined.

****

Shareef had been with Jamal for a month by the time I arrived. In his 20s, Shareef had been displaced to Sana'a from Saada during the conflict. His elder brother had been a staunch Saleh supporter and, Shareef proudly claimed, a member of the Riyadh Dialogue Congress. This was quite ironic for someone who had been so closely aligned with Saleh, but it did illustrate the fluidity of Yemeni politics.

In general, Shareef was happy and often sang. I said that he was good enough to be a famous singer, at which Jamal looked askance at me and said that he would never be a singer because it was considered a lowly profession in tribal areas. Shareef nodded in agreement.

Shareef had been told he would soon be released, although he hadn't been given a specific date. This went on for three weeks. He said several times a day – whether asked or not – that this uncertainty didn't bother him at all, but it clearly did.

Shareef was full of stories, which ranged from bragging about his ability to charm girls to the military expertise of his elder brother. He once told us about the destruction of his family's home in Saada by the Houthis years earlier. The Houthis were infamous for forcing people to leave their homes before dynamiting them. This was punishment for anyone who sided with Saleh, as Shareef's brother had. Anyway, according to him, a few months after his family had moved to another house, they had a visit from the commander who had destroyed their home.

Shareef and his brothers were armed and on the roof, waiting for him to come close enough for them to take their revenge. He described the event, imitating his father as he implored them: "No, no, no, my sons, not now! Later, later, his time will come later!"

I laughed at the way Shareef imitated his father, and mimicked him, asking Shareef to say it again, laughing together.

For many years, Shareef's family had been fighting against the Houthis in Saada. Saleh was still president when Shareef's family was displaced to Sana'a, and they remained loyalists as long as Saleh stood up against the Houthis.

Shareef did not participate in the anti-Saleh protests but instead went to the counter-demonstrations, marches and sit-ins, and he described how he accepted money, food and gifts from the organisers.

During the Arab Spring, it was a standard joke that these counter-demonstrations were phony and the participants had been paid in order to create the appearance of public support for the regime. Meanwhile, those of us at the opposition demonstrations made great personal sacrifices and received no payment!

After Saleh was overthrown in 2011 and formed an alliance with the Houthis in 2014, Shareef's family switched allegiances, supporting General Ali Mohsen. Unlike Saleh, they would never side with those responsible for demolishing their home. They wanted revenge.

For days, I would mimic his father saying "No, no, no, not now!", which would make Shareef roar with laughter.

He also told us that his brother had attended magyal of both ex-president Saleh and General Mohsen and had been able to enjoy friendly conversations with both men. They were ambitious and would happily accept money from both sides. Between 2012 and 2014, this was the nature of politics in the capital, where rival authorities operated in the same territory.

Shareef once described how the former president had pointedly asked his brother if Mohsen also gave him money.

"I wish it was so," his brother had apparently replied, "but you have so badly battered all of these '*ashab al-rabe'a*' [supporters of the Arab Spring] that they can't feed themselves, let alone pay me."

Saleh laughed at this reply and kept joking about it for the next hour, but it is a story that perfectly illustrates Saleh's sway even after his removal as president. It also shows how tribesmen moved freely and easily between political foes depending on who was offering handouts. By this means, Saleh retained a well-functioning network of spies who kept him informed about the balance of power.

On the one occasion when he accompanied his brother to a *magyal*, Shareef dared to ask Saleh for financial assistance.

"We can hardly make ends meet," he had said, "and it would be nice if you could help us so that we don't seek it in other ways".

The following day a bag filled with 800,000 rials (roughly USD2,500 in those days) arrived, but his brother would not give him any, claiming Saleh would have sent it whether or not Shareef had asked. He also told us that the bag had originally held one million riyals, before Saleh's lackeys had snatched a share for themselves – but that was "just how things are done", according to Shareef.

The coup staged by Saleh and his Houthi allies forced Shareef and his brother to contemplate their own next move. General Mohsen fled into exile in Saudi Arabia, not long before President Abdrabbuh Mansur Hadi, after his house arrest in January 2015 and a brief stay the following month in Aden.

According to Shareef, it was in late March 2015, when the Saudis began Operation Decisive Storm, that his brother decided to follow Mohsen to Saudi Arabia, where he joined the armed forces under President Hadi's leadership.

Chapter 8

As the days passed with no sign of his release, Shareef was clearly becoming increasingly distressed. Although he did his best not to show it, I could see the anxiety taking its toll. Our jailers knew the effect that this mix of despair and anticipation had on prisoners and made use of it.

Jamal and Shareef would whisper to each other, often for hours. Jamal mainly gave instructions about the favours Shareef would do for him after his release. Because Shareef was from Saada, he was acquainted with influential Houthis who now ruled Sana'a. They often discussed the best ways to bribe them. By this point, it was common knowledge that the Houthis were as corrupt as Saleh's regime, if not more so.

One evening an armed soldier dressed in National Security uniform opened the cell door and ordered Shareef out. He quickly changed into a clean thobe that he kept pressed under his pillow and slipped out without saying goodbye.

For days, Jamal was incensed at this. He had at least expected a hug and farewell kiss after all their time together. I, on the other hand, took it as a demonstration that uniformed authority often made people meek and passive. This can be true even of those who regard themselves as tough and resilient.

I felt sorry for Jamal but didn't try to cheer him with empty words. I dislike those who seek to reassure me that everything will be alright in the end, so I did not want to offer illusions myself. I usually had little sympathy for those who cried, but if there was no one else to console them, I would. But generally speaking, I neither encouraged nor discouraged my fellow inmates.

In jail, optimism was dangerous, but pessimism was worse; while the former might be helpful in the short run, the latter served no purpose. I had seen the toll that false optimism could take and didn't like it. I only demanded of myself that I endure the ordeal, formulating for myself a daily regimen of exercise, contemplation and stoicism.

An hour or so after Shareef's abrupt departure, his place was taken by a young boy, whose graceful movement impressed me. Jamal asked him the usual questions: name, age, hometown and why he had been arrested. The lad told us he was called Naji, was 14 years old, from Khawlan Al-Tiyal, and that he'd been accused of being a member of Al-Qaeda. He came from the desert plains of Marib, east of the capital, and was a member of the Khawlan tribe, one of the biggest groupings of the Bakeel tribal confederation. But he insisted he was not Al-Qaeda.

When the Saudi air strikes started, he had been taken from his home to join President Hadi's forces in Marib, despite his age. Naji did not expand on this and we didn't ask, because these were sensitive matters and there could be consequences if interrogators knew about it. He said he took leave from his brigade during Ramadan to pay a surprise visit to his family. His father was delighted to see him and sent him to Sana'a in a battered pickup to buy holiday clothes and treats for his siblings for the Eid festivities with his three-months-worth of pay. But when he arrived in the capital, he was picked up by the Houthis. Apparently, there was an informer in his village.

"Does your family know you're here?" I whispered.

"No," he answered quietly, before excusing himself to perform ablutions in the corner before his Isha prayer. He had been unable to pray the previous night as he had been busy with the interrogators.

I was astonished to see him pray in an orthodox Sunni style – standing with arms folded over his midriff – despite coming from a traditional Zaydi area. Nevertheless, he repeated the supplication like an educated Sunni; clearly, he had been given lessons in Quranic recitation and had absorbed them well.

Towards midnight, a guard suddenly opened the cell door and ordered Naji out. Realising that he was being sent for more interrogation, he quickly slipped into a clean, well-pressed *thobe*, wanting to appear at his best. I had never seen anyone so concerned about their appearance during questioning.

Jamal concluded that Naji had studied in one of the Sunni religious institutes that had been opened across Yemen with Saudi and Gulf funding to spread Sunni customs and practices through the Zaydi heartlands. This campaign was initiated by a supposed religious scholar called Abdul Majeed Al-Zindani – a man I considered a fake scholar and a quack doctor who used Islamic teachings to offer spurious 'medical' advice. He claimed to have discovered treatments for viral hepatitis, AIDS and diabetes and sold counterfeit remedies to the gullible. I had often treated people whose condition had deteriorated after replacing their (admittedly more expensive) medication with his fake potions.

When Naji returned, he described being asked to identify a series of photos of bearded men – none of whom he had recognised. Jamal was impressed by the boy's manners and knowledge but didn't want him sharing our cell, so he convinced Naji to complain to the guards that he wasn't strong enough to help care for a paralysed man and should be replaced by a stronger person.

He did as he was told, as if it had been his own idea. The guard found the boy receptive and he was moved that very night, to be replaced by a bigger, brawnier prisoner called Sultan. But Naji had left me with much to contemplate.

Chapter 9

S ultan, a tall, decent man, told us about his two-day interrogation at National Security headquarters three months earlier. He had been invited by his cousin to accompany him on an errand to Sana'a. Sultan jumped at the chance because he was keen to see a nurse he'd fallen in love with when visiting his sister in the capital's maternity hospital the year before. He had kept in touch with the nurse on Facebook and wanted to marry her. He had had some difficulties with her brother, but eventually the woman's family agreed that he could ask for her hand in marriage.

His interrogator had asked Sultan why he hadn't tried to marry someone from his own region, Marib, to which he had replied that it was too expensive: the bride's dowry alone would have cost him five million rials, a sum he couldn't afford. Sultan's interrogators were apparently enthralled by his love story and wanted all the details, laughing as much as Jamal and I did when he told us the tale. We laughed partly because the events had ended up with him sitting with us in a grim prison cell, and partly because of the skilful way he told his story in a charming Bedouin accent.

He described how his cousin's car had been searched at every checkpoint on the way to Sana'a, culminating in their arrest at the last one before the capital on the pretext that explosives had been found hidden underneath the chassis.

"They handcuffed us but didn't show us any explosives," he told us, "so I asked the interrogators, 'How on earth is that? How can they find explosives but not show us?' The interrogators began laughing when I begged to know how they could search our car at more than a dozen checkpoints but only find the explosives at the last one."

Sultan said that his interrogators were still laughing when they finished questioning him for the day. The next day he was brought back before the same two men, who continued with a similar line of questioning. But this time it was no laughing matter. One of them punched him on the jaw and hit him again each time he tried to answer, demanding a different explanation from him.

Sultan had worked as a night security guard for an oil company in Marib, looking after a pipeline in the desert. Local tribesmen were often employed on tasks like this – jobs that weren't really necessary but were offered in exchange for a halt in tribal attacks on the oil companies. The government was incapable of providing protection in heavily armed tribal regions, so instead the protagonists would settle for this arrangement in which they would offer employment in return for peace. In Yemen this counted as petty corruption as opposed to the major corruption involving commissions, contracts, local licensing and other big deals that went exclusively to Saleh, his family and loyalists.

Sultan described his experiences as a night watchman in the desert. One day, his supervisor asked him to go to a certain checkpoint he had never served at before. The site had a one-room concrete shelter he could use when not outside checking the pipeline. On one occasion, he had heard hissing and voices from inside and was certain that it was coming from a genie.

"If I'd known that all the other guards had refused to go there on account of the *djinn*, I wouldn't have gone!" he told us.

Sultan was a fabulous storyteller, especially when he talked about genies, a popular subject throughout Yemen. The Bedouin are famously eloquent with their use of classical Arabic words and traditional phrases, and Jamal and I really enjoyed listening to him. Even so, I told Sultan that I was possibly the only person in the prison who didn't believe in genies. He was, of course, determined to convince me that his encounter was real.

Sultan warned the genie to leave the shelter 'or else', but the eerie sounds continued. He aimed his Kalashnikov at the building and fired off an entire magazine of bullets. At this the noises from inside stopped, but he still did not dare to go in, instead spending the night shivering outside. In the morning all he could find were the bullet marks in the walls. Both he and Jamal gave me a knowing look, as if the story proved the existence of genies.

"How silly!" I said, trying to suppress my laughter. "Couldn't your genie find a better use for its supernatural abilities than to haunt a night watchman at some remote spot in the desert?"

The two gave me a look that said *I* was silly not to believe that a genie could haunt the desert night.

I took out the worn toothbrush I had been using for two months. When Sultan noticed that I brushed only with water, he pulled out a hidden tube of toothpaste and gave it to me to keep. I thought this was incredibly generous and thanked him profusely. Over the next two months, I carefully rationed it to make the small tube last as long as possible.

Sultan begged the guards to move him into his cousin's cell, but this was always denied. The two men only saw each other in the prison yard. Each time they would chat and laugh without pause.

Of the three of us, I was the only *ra'eiyah* – a subject of the old imamate system. Historically, *ra'eiyah* were unarmed because they did not believe in fighting. By contrast, both Jamal and Sultan were tribesmen accustomed to fighting for what they wanted.

Jamal would often proudly tell stories about mountain battles he had been in. He insisted to Sultan that the tribesmen of the northern mountains were much better warriors than tribes from Marib because the latter couldn't 'jump' into battle so well. In other words, they weren't able to concentrate forces at strategic points of a battlefield. Sultan reluctantly conceded this point but insisted that northern tribesmen would not stand a chance if they faced Marib tribesmen in the desert. In the end the two of them agreed that northerners would triumph in mountain skirmishes and Bedouins in desert fighting.

I followed their debates, thinking what it meant to live in a country where people burdened by centuries of grudges live in such varied landscapes. Yemen is breathtakingly beautiful. It ranges from wide deserts to deep canyons, from fertile volcanic valleys with subtropical jungles to tall mountain peaks where snow falls during the winter.

Throughout history, Yemen has been famed as a land difficult for any single group to control, and nearly impossible for outsiders to occupy. Yemenis like to think of their land as 'the graveyard of empires', much as the people of Afghanistan believe. There are few places on earth more rugged and inaccessible than Yemen – perhaps the Hindu Kush, Tibet and parts of central Africa. But in the Middle East, Yemen is without equal. When Arab tribes go to war, their battles resemble a game of chequers. But when Yemeni tribes go to war, they play three-dimensional chess.

People like me simply want to live in peace and to raise the standard of living for everyone in the country. It truly is a shame that a country as beautiful as Yemen has to endure the tragedy of repeated conflict fuelled by old grudges.

When I told Sultan about a visit to Marib I had made in the mid-1970s, he said that it was very different now. Fruit farms were everywhere, but the local people generally didn't work in them. Instead, the land was leased by wealthy landowners and sheikhs who built themselves huge, luxurious houses on their vast ranches and brought in labourers to work for them.

In the 1980s, the desert of Marib was restored to fertility when Sheikh Zayid bin Nahyan, the ruler of the UAE, invested tens of millions of dollars to build a new dam near the site of the ancient Great Marib Dam. Sheikh Zayid claimed that his ancestors had migrated from Marib, so he felt honoured to contribute to the region's economic development in tribute to his family's legacy.

The truth is that large segments of the Arab population around the world today can trace their lineage back to Marib because, in its day, the city was the largest on the Arabian Peninsula.

I was fascinated as I listened to Sultan's tales about Marib. He described how tribesmen travelled deep into the desert after the rainy season to graze their flocks of goats and camels. He promised that he would arrange such an experience for me after we were released.

****

Whenever the water supply ran out, Sultan was quick to get the latest gossip and news. Jamal was often displeased with the news Sultan relayed to us and when his patience ran short, he would take Sultan's place, believing that he could get better news than anyone else from our 'switchboard'. After asking one or two questions about the latest news, though, he would turn his attention to getting hold of Tareq Al-Ma'eili, the dream interpreter. If he was successful, it was his lucky day and he would squat under the tap describing his latest dreams, listening carefully to every word Tareq uttered.

Sultan's main concern was to be moved to his cousin's cell, but he also enjoyed talking to the guards through the hatch. He would often repeat the funny story about his capture, but about his freedom he would say to me: "Doctor, you and I won't be released because both of us were arrested because of our regional backgrounds".

Sultan stayed with us for a month, much of which he spent asleep – once for 20 hours in a single day. Jamal passed the time reading the Quran, while I spent most of mine exercising and thinking.

Chapter 10

When Sultan moved out, he was replaced by Mu'ataz Al-Suri from Syria, who had been in the neighbouring cell. He was raised in Saudi Arabia, where his father was an Arabic teacher. His ambition was to become a doctor but, after being refused by Saudi medical schools, he came to Sana'a to study medicine and he had been addressed as 'Doctor' ever since.

He became fluent in English thanks to an American girlfriend who had offered to take him back with her to the US; but by then he was more interested in business and was finding it easy to make money in Sana'a thanks to his online research skills and language ability. However, his activities brought him into the orbit of some shady characters – including arms dealers – and during the interim government he became involved with the Minister of Defence, Mohammad Nasser.

Before his arrest, Mu'ataz worked for an American former employee of the US Embassy who was involved in building the jail in which we were now incarcerated. It had originally been funded by the US government, which wanted a high-security prison to hold Al-Qaeda detainees. At this time, President Saleh's nephew, Ammar Muhammad Saleh, was the director of National Security.

When the Houthis took control of Sana'a airport, Mu'ataz's boss was arrested after he tried to re-enter the country. He was accused of spying and a substantial ransom put on his head. Shortly after this, Mu'ataz was also arrested on the same charge, badly beaten and thrown into a cell with Al-Qaeda members.

"They wanted Al-Qaeda to finish what the interrogators started," he claimed. "They told them I worked as a spy for an American. But instead of killing me, they cleaned my wounds and looked after me until I recovered. It was actually fun staying with Al-Qaeda. With a few dates, they could make a good fermented home brew."

I was amazed – Al-Qaeda are meant to be strict Muslims.

"It's *halal* to ferment grapes or dates for two and a half days," he explained. "The Prophet himself used to have such drinks."

Of course, I knew this and that making alcohol had been around since ancient times. But did the drink have any effect on them, I asked.

"Not much, but it made them laugh more than usual," he said.

Jamal was more interested in talking business with Mu'ataz, offering to use his tribal and partisan connections to get government contracts if Mu'ataz would find the best bargains with companies abroad. Jamal boasted that he knew how the system worked and stressed the need for both 'carrot and stick'. They both discussed offers one could not afford to refuse.

We listened to the coalition fighters flying over Sana'a. From time to time, huge explosions reverberated through our cell. But apparently money was more captivating to my cellmates. What this says about human nature was remarkable to me.

Despite the destruction of the country, man's capacity to dream never ceased and, as long as dreams existed among inmates in a prison, there was determination to keep hoping for a better future. My cellmates clearly believed they would do better in business than before their arrest.

In a philosophical mood one day, Mu'ataz stared at me and said he believed that I was treating my imprisonment as an experiment or experience and that I seemed eager to take it all in. I didn't ask him to explain what he meant and just responded with a smile.

I certainly suffered from the ordeal of captivity, but I tried to detach myself from the miserable circumstances as if watching from above. I believed that whatever happened inside prison fitted within a greater context of events and that the ongoing tragedy in Yemen reflected a pattern of individual and group grudges, rivalries and conflicts that had been repeated throughout history.

I was determined not to give my jailers the satisfaction of breaking my spirit. Yes, I sat in a dark jail cell with little light, fresh air or adequate food, but my spirit was always free to fly into heaven above.

****

The head jailer, Abu Shamekh, developed a liking for Mu'ataz. They got along in a very strange way. When Mu'ataz was in his previous cell, he began a hunger strike and the jailers were forced to contact Abu Shamekh, who was on vacation at the time. Thereafter, the two of them frequently chatted and joked whenever Abu Shamekh appeared at the hatch.

One day, Abu Shamekh appeared there looking sad and shaking his head. Without explanation, he said to Mu'ataz: "From the bottom of my heart, I wish to be a martyr." Then he vanished as quickly as he had appeared.

"A donkey martyr," I murmured in the silence of our cell. Jamal laughed because he hated Abu Shamekh, who was particularly rude to him. "A brave warrior would sacrifice himself in a battle but shouldn't actually wish to die for the sake of becoming a martyr," I continued.

Jamal laughed again and said that Abu Shamekh's wish was probably the result of a Saudi air strike that had killed some Houthis.

Later, when Jamal used the water pipes, he told Tareq the nickname I had coined for Abu Shamekh. Tareq, the local Al-Qaeda kingpin who usually inspired fear and awe, laughed at 'the donkey martyr' and asked Jamal to pass on his warm regards to me.

****

The first time I learned about Al-Qaeda's presence in the prison was before the call to dawn prayer one day, when I heard what sounded like the distant buzz of bees. Jamal told me it was Al-Qaeda prisoners reciting verses from the Quran. One jailer tried to get them to shut up, but he couldn't really order an inmate to stop reciting the holy text.

There was no love lost between Al-Qaeda and the jailers, who in fact were afraid of them. There were many instances outside the prison of security personnel being assassinated because of their treatment of Al-Qaeda prisoners, so most jailers wore masks to protect their identity.

Soon after Jamal told me the buzzing came from Al-Qaeda members, I heard the *athan*, the call to prayer, made beautifully by a pious Al-Qaeda prisoner. This was on my eighth day in jail, when Shareef was still in the cell with me and Jamal.

"You'll see them when we go outside," Shareef said.

We were meant to be allowed outside for some fresh air and sunlight once a week, but the jailers often changed their minds on a whim. One Tuesday morning we heard the shouts that signalled we were to be let out. For some this meant a frantic rush to hide their possessions from the guards, who would search the cells while we were out. But I had nothing, so I had a quick pee in preparation for my first trip out of the cell in 10 days. I hadn't seen direct daylight, let alone the sun, since I was kidnapped from my home.

I was led from the cell barefoot, blindfolded and chained to another prisoner. Amid rude, deafening shouts from the guards, we were ordered to stay in line and remain silent. The companion I was chained to meekly asked a guard what day it was, but the guard snarled back, naming the wrong day, just for the sake of being vindictive. I made a point of noting the date each morning so that I knew exactly how much time passed. For the first few weeks, I even coined a name for each day after reviewing what had happened.

The practice of blindfolding and chaining inmates is so humiliating. But I could not allow myself to show feelings of contempt. It filled me with anger to hear the guard name the wrong day of the week because it showed how jailers could be manipulative just for the sake of it. Instead of speaking my mind, I translated the feelings inside me into an intense desire that all the jailers would one day be held accountable and made to pay for what they did to us.

The doorway into the sun yard was elevated but there were no stairs down to the ground. The jailers placed several cinder blocks to serve as steps. Not just because we were barefoot, blindfolded and tied to each other, it was tricky going down as the blocks moved and rocked under our feet. They gave us directions, shouting, "Mind the step, mind the door," yet some of us still fell to the ground.

We walked round the corner of the building and then the guards removed our blindfolds. The sun-baked yard was full of stones and surrounded by high stone walls, half in sunlight, half in shadow. We couldn't see anything of the outside world, apart from a small patch of sky. I could see a circle of prisoners, exchanging greetings and chatting. I was still chained and didn't know if I should be more frightened of the jailers or the Al-Qaeda prisoners.

Other inmates greeted the man I was chained to and I realised from their comments that he was Jewish. I was eager to feel the sun's rays, but he didn't like sun so tried to pull me towards the shade as I tugged him towards the sun. We were ordered not to remain standing, but my companion refused to sit, so I sat in the sun while chained to him as he stood in the shade. The jailers ordered him to sit, and when he refused they sent him back to his cell, so they unchained me from him and instead chained me to Jamal and Shareef, who were sitting nearby.

At first, I didn't realise it was them because they looked quite different in the bright sunlight after so long in a dim cell. I was embarrassed to not recognise them instantly and worried that my eyesight or my mind was fading from my time in jail.

I continued to examine the faces and the surroundings. One inmate caught my eye and asked where I was from, and I told him; another asked what I had done and I made a gesture of holding a pen to imply that I was arrested for writing.

A third person shouted: "Are you a journalist?"

"No, a doctor of medicine," I replied, to their evident surprise.

I had expected them to be afraid of the jailers, but instead they cracked jokes about them. The inmates from Aden were particularly vocal, but they paid dearly for the jokes later on; I never saw them mock the jailers after that.

"Boys with *tayyihni* trousers humiliated Houthi militiamen and Saleh's tribal soldiers," a prisoner called Rami said to Abu Basheer. (*Tayyihni* are low-slung jeans favoured by many adolescents.) Others joined in, saying how 'good-for-nothing' youngsters from Aden had been able to give the Houthis a bloody nose.

An Al-Qaeda prisoner was animatedly recounting how Taiz had proved Saleh wrong.

"Saleh used to say he could tame Taiz with a handful of soldiers armed with a few sticks," he said, "but the youth of Taiz have delivered a knock-out blow to his troops. Without any military training they managed to rub their noses in the dirt."

The jailers reacted to the ribbing with timorous grins and nods. They were mainly from the north, so were meant to be offended by the jokes. During my incarceration, I met only two jailers who weren't northern tribesmen – these two being 'black sheep' from Taiz.

For half an hour, I absorbed every word spoken and every gesture made as I quietly enjoyed the sunlight and fresh air. Then Jamal nudged me and began whispering, pointing out who was Al-Qaeda and who wasn't. There were about 30 Al-Qaeda members among the 50 of us in the yard.

Two hours in the sun passed in no time before we were ordered to our feet and marched back to our cells, two-by-two. As one pair passed me, one of them leaned down to kiss the top of my head and told me that he was proud of being both a Hashemite and an Al-Qaeda member.

This was unheard of: Al-Qaeda is supposedly the most extreme Sunni position, while Yemeni Hashemites are nominally Shia. The Houthi family is Hashemite, so a Hashemite Al-Qaeda leader locked in a Houthi jail was an apparent contradiction.

Kissed on the head by this Al-Qaeda bigwig, I realised that I had been accepted by a group of prisoners who were intensely anti-Houthi and anti-Saleh. And being a doctor from Taiz made me especially popular.

On the way back to our cells, I entertained a pleasant thought. I wanted to make use of the warmth I had absorbed to wash my entire body. Usually, our water was too cold to wash thoroughly, but when I returned to the cell that day I was able to strip and bathe fully. It wasn't great – I had no towel and had to dress again in my grubby jeans and T-shirt, but nevertheless I was reasonably clean for only the second time since I'd been arrested.

Chapter 11

During my time in jail, I lost three fillings, one from a tooth that had previously required root canal treatment. This was when I was sharing a cell with Jamal and Mu'ataz. Unsurprisingly, the guards were indifferent to my pleas to see a dentist, so I stopped eating because of the discomfort and my fear of infection.

When Mu'ataz told Abu Shamekh about my plight, he said he couldn't care less if I died – a sentiment that the guards took pleasure in repeating. After 36 hours or so, I began to eat a little without chewing, and eventually I stopped worrying about infection and finally began eating regularly again. It always felt like a contest between me and the jailers – and I was determined to score more points.

Jamal once said to me that the only way I would be released was if my friend Sheikh Hamoud Al-Mikhlafi, the resistance leader in Taiz, captured a *qandeel* who could be exchanged for me.

I also had a pet name for Houthi leader Abdulmalek Al-Houthi: 'Schizoid', because of his delusional notions. He would often talk about the apocalypse and believed that he was carrying out God's will, quoting religious texts foretelling the liberation of Makkah and Jerusalem, which would come at the hands of Al-Mansour ('The Victorious' – meaning him), who would arrive from the south (meaning Yemen).

It was widely assumed that he was safely hidden in caves in the Marran mountains of Saada governorate. From here, he could not witness the destruction caused by the war against the Saudi coalition, which he described as an enemy of Islam, but he kept claiming to be winning. Like other Islamists, he promised that any supporter who died a martyr's death would be rewarded in heaven by beautiful female angels who would fulfil every desire.

I knew there was no chance of negotiating peace with such a man. He believed he was entitled to rule as a direct descendant of the Prophet and was achieving his dream as a sayyid. And, on a more worldly level, he had developed a taste for wealth, luxury and power, which he wouldn't give up.

The Houthis believe in *tamkeen* (empowering), meaning that God is enabling them to carry out impossible missions, to overcome formidable enemies and to benefit from services from the most unlikely sources, such as the British and the Americans.

They also believe that victory comes by the hand of God and believe themselves invincible, since Al-Houthi is the 'Chosen One'. Furthermore, they are prepared to inflict ruin on Yemen because cost has no meaning when one is fighting for God. Another factor that makes them reluctant to reach a peaceful solution is that they know Yemenis would like to avenge themselves for the atrocities inflicted upon them. And the clincher is that they are allied to Tehran, which so far has blocked all potential moves towards peace.

Chapter 12

One night we were woken by the sound of running feet in the corridor. Minutes later, our door burst open and I was ordered out. Jamal and Mu'ataz had immediately sensed it was about an attempted suicide in the jail. I wondered why they thought this, but, unfortunately, they were right. I was hurried to an upper floor to examine the poor inmate who had taken this desperate action. It was the first time I had been outside the cell without a blindfold and handcuffs.

The following night when the water pipes were empty, the incident was the talk of our secret switchboard. Adel from the neighbouring cell asked Mu'ataz whether it was *sha* or *mash* (*shanq* means hanging and *mashrat* means cutting the wrists). In our society, suicide elicits scorn, not sympathy, as it is unequivocally haram to end one's own life.

Mu'ataz replied to Adel with the name of the poor man who was a '*sha*'. Nothing else needed to be said. All our fellow prisoners had guessed correctly why I had been summoned. They had also worked out that the man had been unsuccessful, because I had been needed. To my knowledge, there had been more than 10 attempted suicides, three of them successful.

****

I had come to love our secret communications network. Despite being kept in the dark – literally and figuratively – we all knew what was going on. All the 'switchboard operators' would use a code name so they couldn't be identified by the guards. This generally worked and kept the information flowing. But sometimes the operators could be suspicious of who was on the other end of the 'line', thinking that a guard might be eavesdropping. In that case, they would end the conversation instantly.

Of course, the jailers did know about it, and tried to catch us red-handed, occasionally keeping the pipes empty to tempt us, and then trying to creep up on us and catch us in the act. But the sharp ears of the inmates could usually pick up the slightest sound from the corridors, thwarting their ambushes.

On our trips to the yard, we would often be lectured about this by Abu Basheer, the commandant.

"Chatting is forbidden, and anyone caught will be severely punished," he warned us. The usual punishment would be to deprive us of water for days on end. And although this did increase the use of the switchboard, cutting off the water was terrible since we couldn't wash and were continually thirsty. Not being able to wash for prayers was much worse than not being able to communicate.

Nevertheless, our communication system was a popular source of amusement as we would share rumours and try to work out what was happening both inside and outside the prison. The guessing game could become very tricky with some overplaying the game, making huge gaffes based on ridiculous assumptions.

"Say that again," I always asked any good-natured person who had offered an unlikely bit of speculation. Ill-tempered correspondents were another matter entirely. Their malicious gossip caused a great deal of unnecessary stress. I wouldn't have anything to do with such people and could easily dismiss them from my thoughts. This was an important defence mechanism.

To have people like that around was torment. Dealings with certain jailers could cause a short, sharp burst of distress, but having an ill-tempered cellmate was a source of constant anguish. Even if relations began well enough, they could soon sour in such crowded conditions.

All relationships have an expiry date, I thought, which set me thinking about an American movie I had once seen, *The War of the Roses*, a black comedy about a disintegrating marriage. Indeed, recalling scenes from movies was something I often did to escape the misery and boredom of prison life. Fantasy films were best, and once I even managed to transport myself elsewhere for 36 continuous hours. But then I began to worry that I was losing my grip, so forced myself to return to the reality of a miserable, squalid jail cell.

****

One night, I started to feel nauseous. I really didn't want to fall ill in jail, the worst place on earth for it to happen. The jailers couldn't care less about one's suffering and would often enjoy our agonies. On this occasion, it was the worst colic I had ever experienced. I couldn't eat or move, so I tried to stay as still as I could and suffer in silence.

I couldn't understand what was wrong. My abdomen was rigid and tender, every movement painful. What could it be? Then the pain shot to my back. Could it be pancreatitis or a perforated gut? I didn't eat for the next 36 hours, despite my companions encouraging me to take a little nourishment – I was just too nauseous.

After a couple of days, I noticed that when I pressed the tender spots over my ribs, I heard cracking. With relief, I realised it was Tietze syndrome, a rare condition that can be painful but is almost never serious – just very difficult to diagnose. It happens when the cartilage around the joints connecting the upper ribs to the breastbone becomes inflamed.

At the same time, I began to sense discomfort and stiffness in my hips caused by tight iliopsoas muscles (which run from the lower back to the groin and flex the hip joint). This had probably been caused by a combination of overexercise and too much sitting in the cold. Fortunately, knowing what was wrong, I could treat myself by massaging my ribs, varying my stretching exercises and wrapping up warmly when I was sitting, not just when I slept. Gradually, I got better. In hindsight, I had probably been suffering from a peptic ulcer, on top of all the muscular and skeletal aches and pains.

In my professional life, I had taken pride in being able to diagnose Tietze syndrome in patients who had come to me after visiting several other doctors with no success. Although I was in pain, I enjoyed the irony of diagnosing it again with myself as the patient, sitting in prison.

Jamal kindly offered me some sweets made from tahini to take my mind off the discomfort. This was something the jailers brought us most Thursdays. It had been ages since I put something sweet in my mouth. It tasted like heaven, but it also reminded me that I was becoming much too thin.

Chapter 13

When Mu'ataz left our cell, he was replaced by Abu Bara'a, also a Syrian, whose real name was Abd Al-Mu'ezz. He spoke with a heavy northern tribal accent and had been a veterinary student at Dhamar University, south of Sana'a. While his parents had fled Syria to Turkey after fighting erupted between Islamic militant groups, he was arrested in Yemen after having quit his studies to join Al-Qaeda.

I asked him if his mother knew he now had such a strong Yemeni tribal accent.

"Yes, I talked to her over the phone before I joined Al-Qaeda, and my accent showed over my Syrian one."

"And what did she say?"

"*Kharrabuk*! ['They ruined you'']," he laughed. His mother was clearly in agony because she believed he had destroyed his future. I felt sad for her; there's nothing more painful for a parent than to see their child ruined. Nonetheless, it made me laugh to know that she could tell exactly what Yemen had done to her son by his new accent.

"You could have at least finished university and kept your options open for the future," I said.

His face turned serious as he replied: "People like you have chosen the material life – you want to live better, eat better and have children. People like me will always choose the afterlife. It's a win-win situation for us. If we live a long life, we'll serve God more. If we are to die as martyrs, then we go straight to heaven."

It was clear that he thought I was the loser because, by refusing to fight in the name of the Almighty, I wasn't serving God in the 'false' earthly life, so there was no way that I could become a martyr and enjoy paradise.

"But don't you want to have children of your own?" I asked.

"Getting married is easy in Al-Qaeda," he said. "It doesn't cost us one rial. Al-Qaeda is now in control of Hadhramaut, and they will give me a wife upon my release. Al-Qaeda will kidnap soldiers, officials and foreigners and use them to bargain for our release. After that, I can travel to Hadhramaut and be married for free."

I had learned that Al-Qaeda members liked to prove that they were better at logical argument and that someone well-educated was wrong. It was impossible to debate with him because he believed simplistically that people who sought to live a good life on earth were doomed – unlike those such as him, who sought martyrdom through jihad against the supposed enemies of Islam.

Abu Bara'a was completely self-assured, despite sitting in the same miserable jail cell as us. He firmly believed that Al-Qaeda was already in control of Hadhramaut, where its leaders were building what they believed to be a true Islamic state. He was also certain that he would soon be released in exchange for hostages and had no doubt whatsoever that, after he was set free, Al-Qaeda would provide him a wife. He even told me that after having children he would return to jihad, become a martyr and enjoy paradise in the afterlife. Deserting his wife and abandoning his children without a father was apparently not a problem.

****

Al-Qaeda had gained control of two southern regions of Yemen, first establishing a power base in Abyan governorate, north-east of Aden, in 2011, and then in Hadhramaut governorate shortly after the start of Operation Decisive Storm in 2015. Both bore the fingerprints of Saleh's National Security apparatus. Many young men like Abu Bara'a who join Al-Qaeda have no real idea whose agenda they truly serve.

In Abyan, bearded Al-Qaeda fighters occupied the capital, Zinjibar, just a day after a speech by Saleh about the threat posed by Al-Qaeda if the 2011 uprising did not end. His army practically shook hands with the bearded men who took over the city's government offices and checkpoints, occupying the post office and Central Bank and seizing the cash reserves. At the time I tweeted: "Saleh's family army handed Abyan to Saleh's bearded men".

The cordial relationship between the two groups continued until the pro-Saleh General Somali from Sanhan moved his troops to Hadhramaut 18 months later, after which the Abyan Islamic State dissolved without much fuss.

The Hadhramaut Islamic State was even more bizarre and suspicious. Following a jailbreak, the 'beards' seized 40 billion rials (about USD2 billion at the time) from the bank in Al-Mukalla and then proceeded to the city's palace, where their chief posed for a selfie with the presidential flag on a luxurious carpet in the main reception hall. This image immediately appeared across all the media channels. Once again, the rise of Al-Qaeda had happened without a fight, and later it collapsed with a sudden meltdown and withdrawal.

In both incidents, Yemen was smeared with Al-Qaeda's name, inflicting untold harm on the Yemeni people. But the reality would have been so easy to show with a little good journalism; Yemeni Al-Qaeda could be beckoned whenever the man with the money asked them, and they could be passed from one regime to another, moving from bed to bed.

****

In the prison yard one day, Abu Basheer pointed at Abu Bara'a and said to me: "Have you ever seen such a *modber*?"

There is no real English equivalent to that term; it roughly means a jinxed person who inflicts harm or financial loss upon himself because of his poor decisions.

"He's swapped beautiful Syrian girls in this world for virgins in the next," said the commandant, smiling wistfully to himself.

By then Jamal's condition had deteriorated so badly that we had to carry him to do his ablutions. He had become more and more reliant on Abu Bara'a, a responsibility that had begun to wear on the young Syrian. Eventually, he needed a break, so I had to be replaced by a stronger, younger man more able to help with Jamal.

Chapter 14

One evening, I was summoned from the cell to tend sick inmates. Abu Shamekh had become unusually kind to me because he appreciated my willingness to help – something I was more than happy to do, probably because I am both a doctor and a father.

While Abu Shamekh could be rude to the inmates, I sided with them, and he soon realised that I wouldn't be intimidated. I also enjoyed walking the corridors without blindfold or chains. Seeing me walking alongside Abu Shamekh, prisoners would look on with surprise and envy because it was seen as a rare privilege to be allowed to move about freely like this.

Over the course of my medical rounds – which would take place most evenings once Abu Shamekh and the guards had finished their qat sessions – I encountered all sorts of medical complaints.

For instance, I treated a very thin teenaged inmate who was suffering from a discharge of pus from both ears. Abu Shamekh accused him of malingering and ordered him to jump to his feet for some military drills, but I could see he was genuinely sick and persuaded Abu Shamekh to back off. I prescribed antibiotics, ear drops and a thorough cleansing regime, demonstrating what he should do and enlisting the help of his cellmates. A week later I asked Abu Shamekh how the boy was doing, and in an offhand manner he said that headquarters hadn't sent any drugs or swabs, so nothing had changed. I wanted to cry.

Another time I was taken to a dim, crowded cell in which one of the five prisoners was suffering from a severely swollen leg, from groin to toe, and could not stand because of the pain. Seeing evidence of gunshot wounds and a surgical scar in his lower abdomen, I thought he probably had a pelvic deep vein thrombosis that was obstructing the blood flow from his leg. This put him in danger of having a piece of thrombus detach and travel to his lungs, killing him. I advised that he should be immediately sent to a hospital, but, knowing this was unlikely, I also prescribed an anticoagulant and advised him to lie quietly. But neither happened. I was later told that guards advised him to get over his laziness and move around to get better. Sadly, I don't know what happened to him.

There were many such wretched medical cases and Abu Shamekh often made matters worse just by his presence. Nevertheless, many inmates were desperate for my help – even if they didn't always give a full answer to my questions, due to the lack of privacy.

For example, one evening, two men spoke so vaguely about their problem that all I could do was advise them to drink more water. But later on – when they had the opportunity to speak to me in private – I learned that they both had gonorrhoea. On that occasion I managed to convince Abu Shamekh to obtain the necessary drugs, prescribing a longer course of medication than was normal because I did not want to take any chances.

Having heard the circumstances of their illness, the men were devastated when I told them that their wives in all probability needed treatment too. It was one of those sad but all-too-frequent cases in an impoverished city like Sana'a, where poor women were forced to make ends meet by providing sexual services to young men who migrated to the city to find better-paying jobs.

A week later I was pleased to hear that their symptoms had cleared up – but warned them to get checked for syphilis after their release, since symptoms of that condition could be masked by the antibiotics they had taken.

One day, staff from National Security headquarters came to see me about a long list of chronically ill inmates who they wanted me to examine. Over the course of several hours, I visited them all and wrote reports on each of them. A few days later the security men returned with a report I'd written about a prisoner who was partially paralysed. Clearly this had been caused by torture – but my report described the nerve damage without using that word. They demanded I amend my report with a paragraph confirming that I stood by my diagnosis and took full responsibility if it was proved wrong. Angry that they doubted my integrity, I even added that I was willing to pay a fine of one million dollars if I was wrong.

During the last months of my stay in the jail, National Security decided to employ their own doctors, so they dispensed with my services and I reverted to being an ordinary prisoner.

****

One day, after completing my rounds, I asked Abu Shamekh about the Jewish inmate I had met when I had briefly been chained to him in the yard a while before. Afraim was a Yemeni Jew with an Israeli passport who had been arrested by Houthi airport staff when he entered the country. I was intrigued by his story.

"Do you want to meet him again?" Abu Shamekh asked.

I nodded. Ever since I had been a child, I had been fascinated by characters on the margins of society. Even in prison I still retained my childhood curiosity.

My first encounter with a Yemeni Jew had been when I was five years old during the Al-Thulaya rebellion, when the imam killed one of his brothers. The events are still vivid in my memory. My father had brought a poor Jewish worker to our house to make mattresses out of raw cotton. He stayed with us for several days, working all day long in a small room set aside for him. On Saturdays, he shut himself in to observe his sabbath and sent a message to my mother, opening with *amanah*, asking her not to include meat in his meals.

Amanah is a highly regarded concept in Islam, particularly in Yemeni culture. Whenever someone wants something important to them, they begin their request with *amanah*, which signifies it is an almost sacred request that should be granted if at all possible. The Quran says that God requested *amanah* from the mountains, but the mighty mountains could not bear them. When *amanah* was requested from man, he accepted as a sign of man's fallibility.

Of course, my mother was dutifully respectful of the man's *amanah* and would prepare his meals according to kosher rules.

When Abu Shamekh opened the hatch in the door to Afraim's cell, the Jewish inmate jumped to his feet. It was small, so he had only one cellmate, George the Hungarian, who ignored us. Afraim spoke in a Yemeni dialect with a strong northern tribal accent, launching into a long story about how, two years previously, he had left 200,000 rials as *amanah* with a shop owner from Taiz (*amanah* also meaning a surety for safeguarding valuables). Honest people are duty bound to return such *amanah* because it is a great disgrace – and against Islamic teachings – not to do so.

Abu Shamekh listened impatiently before telling Afraim that such a thing was none of his business, so he should upon his release go back to Amran where this happened and report the incident to a *mushref* to get his money back. *Mushrefs* (supervisors) are usually sayyids, most likely from Saada, and are accountable solely to Abdulmalek Al-Houthi, and analogous to a commissar in the Soviet regime.

Abu Shemakh was not interested in the conversation and I was finally able to get Afraim's attention. He knew I was a doctor and, apropos of nothing, he began boasting about Israeli medical expertise.

"Israeli doctors can point a camera towards you and diagnose you immediately," Afraim claimed.

I wasn't in the mood to discuss the brilliant advances of medicine in Israel. Instead, I thought I should exchange a few words with the taciturn Hungarian, who was on his feet intently reading the Quran, treating us as if we didn't exist.

"How's it going, Hakim?" I asked, knowing he preferred to be called by the diminutive of his Muslim name, Abdulhakim.

Speaking fluently in classical Arabic, he replied: "I don't know what's worse, being in jail or being with Afraim. How can someone educated like me be locked up with an ignorant, uneducated man like him?"

Afraim wanted to chat all the time, while George preferred quiet contemplation. As well as his desire to study the Quran, he was also a good baritone and while in jail composed complete operas. For him, being with Afraim was 'hell in a cell'.

After having spoken with Afraim a little, I found my curiosity waning because of his attitude, but I did subsequently learn more about him from a Syrian called Mo'taz Al-Sari, a cellmate in one of the other 15 cells in which I was incarcerated during my 10 months of imprisonment.

The story was that Afraim had earned USD40,000 in dowries from the marriages of his five daughters. Rather than enjoy his money, he wanted to see it grow. Unfortunately for him, the interest rate in banks in Israel, where he was then living, was just one percent – like much of the developed world, but much lower than the three percent offered by the Yemeni Central Bank. Consequently, he decided to deposit his money in Yemen and each year he would travel to Sana'a via Jordan to make sure his deposit was accruing the correct interest payments.

On a visit in 2013, Afraim took a trip to Amran, with a young boy from Sana'a as a guide. They stayed together in a hotel in Amran, where he was accused of sodomy and sentenced to two years in jail. Some months before he was due to be released, the town was stormed by Houthi forces and, amid the chaos, the prison walls were breached and he escaped, eventually fleeing to Israel.

A year later he was back on his annual banking trip, but by now Sana'a was in Houthi hands. He was seen as a potentially valuable hostage, so he was seized immediately after landing and had been in prison ever since.

On a few occasions, I met Afraim in the yard and made an effort to chat to him so he wouldn't feel like such an outcast. But he was very tiresome and always talked about the same thing, insisting that he shouldn't have been put in jail without a trial – something that would never happen in Israel, and in any case, was totally unjust.

I would tell him again that none of this had anything to do with the law, and in all likelihood he would remain there until a ransom had been paid. But my words were always in vain; he would just repeat his usual complaints.

While in the yard, Afraim would often be the subject of abuse from Al-Qaeda prisoners because of his faith. On one occasion, he earned my respect when he stood up to them and silenced their taunts.

"All of you, shut up! Once upon a time you were Jews too! Some Yemenis converted to Christianity and others adopted Islam, but originally we were all Jewish."

He was probably right, too. In what may be an apocryphal tale, a famous Egyptian thinker called Taha Hussein describes in his 1925 book *Hadith Al-Arbi'ah* ("Wednesday Conversations") Judaism's arrival in Yemen like this:

One day, Tobba'a, a king of Yemen during the time of ancient Rome, was traveling through the countries north of his realm, conquering every town along the way when, on reaching the outskirts of Makkah, he came across two rabbis who warned him not to attack Makkah, which was divinely protected. Heeding their warning, Tobba'a bypassed the city and continued on his way north, plundering and conquering as he went. But on his way back, he met the same two men, converted to Judaism himself, and invited the rabbis to come with him and convert Yemen to Judaism.

It is not known exactly when the country converted to Judaism, and how long this remained the state religion, but many historians support what Afraim said. For example, Kamal Salibi, a prominent Lebanese Christian historian, in his 1985 book *The Bible Came from Arabia*, asserts that the original Hebrews actually came from Yemeni lands, believing that the similarity between the names of places throughout Yemen and places recorded in the Torah supports this.

Salibi's theory is that the Babylonian ruler Nebuchadnezzar invaded Yemen and took the original Jews back as slaves. A sizeable portion of the Torah was written down by descendants of the captive Jews, in which they referred to the original names of tribes and mountains in Arabia. Two centuries later, when the Jews of Babylon were liberated, they briefly returned to the lands of their ancestors before eventually wandering northwards and settling in Palestine, naming places there after those in their ancient homeland.

Mu'ataz from Syria told me that, when they shared a cell, Afraim would always ask him to recite from the Quran, being particularly fond of Surat Al-Baqarah (The Cow), which tells the story of Moses leading his people in their flight from Egypt. Mu'ataz would also give him regular massages to ease his backache. As a sign of his gratitude, Afraim offered to do something for Mu'ataz after their release.

"Allow me to marry one of your daughters," Mu'ataz requested.

"All five have already been married, and they live in London, New York and Israel," said Afraim. "But I can help you to marry one of the Yemeni rabbi's beautiful daughters."

This struck me as a most unusual offer since it was exceptional for a Yemeni Jew to marry across faiths since it would diminish their community.

During my time in prison, there were negotiations between the Houthis, the US, Oman and Israel to arrange safe passage for Jews from Sana'a who wanted to leave for Israel. When Afraim was eventually released, it was presumably as part of this grand deal.

****

Around the same time as my dealings with Afraim, I was sitting in the yard when a group of four men appeared, all chained together. This turned out to be Abbood, a tall, strong ex-soldier who had subsequently joined Al-Qaeda, with the Fadhli brothers and a man called Yaf'ei. These three were also considered to be Al-Qaeda.

Before sitting, they shook hands and kissed the cheeks of every inmate in the circle. One of the Fadhli boys carried a plastic bottle of water, which made me curious as plastic bottles were forbidden in the jail. I was told that an evil spirit dwelt inside Abbood. He was kept chained to his cellmates because he was known to turn violent. I was also told that the water in the bottle was not just any water, but holy water ('holy' because the boys would read verses and suras from the Quran into a water-filled plastic bottle, close it tightly and put it safely in a corner until it was needed).

One Tuesday, Abbood suddenly started to writhe and roar incoherently, pulling his compatriots about with him. Everyone presumed this was because of the angry demon inside him. This continued for some time, his cellmates struggling to restrain him. The boy who held the bottle with anti-genie spells couldn't open it because of the violent movement, which disappointed me because I wanted to see what the magic water would do when sprinkled on him.

Most of the prisoners and guards seemed frightened, but for me it was their reactions that were more frightening than the 'demon genie' itself. Eventually, Abbood knelt and started to wretch violently, all eyes upon him. He had little in his stomach to throw up – just a little yellow bile – but when someone saw a clump of hair in his vomit, a gasp went up. There was surely no better evidence than this that an angry spirit lived within him!

Finally, as the act approached its end, the boy managed to sprinkle Abbood with the water to quieten him. The pool of vomit became the centre of attention. Even the commandant was staring, before silently beckoning one of his guards to cover it with soil and pebbles.

In fact, ingesting one's own hair is a rare medical condition called trichobezoar, often suffered by people with personality disorders but also sometimes a symptom of malingering. However, I had been surprised by the violence of his contractions, which made him bring up not just his stomach juices but also the yellow bile that came from deep in the duodenum. I told the commandant that I could treat Abbood.

Everyone else looked at me with ridicule, but the commandant stared and gave me a faint nod.

I tried to explain my medical diagnosis later in our cell to Jamal and Mu'ataz, but of course they wouldn't have it – my scientific explanation was not nearly as convincing as their superstitions. They were in a mood to educate me about the relationship between humans and genies. Jamal had a degree in humanities and Mu'ataz graduated in medicine. Nevertheless, Jamal asserted that, because the Quran mentions the existence of genies, there was nothing further to discuss, while Mu'ataz told me stories about possessed inmates he had come across.

One genie had apparently made an inmate dance and sing in a foreign language that the man had not known. Another 'possessed' inmate had talked eloquently about a scholastic subject he had never studied. According to Mu'ataz, if the inmates were able to speak in languages or discuss topics that were impossible to know, the only explanation was that there was a genie inside them.

Being a medical school graduate, Mu'ataz could appreciate my scientific explanations for both Abbood and the other stories of possession. He even liked what I said, but he didn't dare approve or agree. He was a very polite person who tried to help everyone in the prison in whatever way possible.

On another occasion I was in a cell with a youngster from Al-Qaeda who tried to convince me that possession by genies was normal.

"Everyone is possessed by genies," he said. "Even people like you who aren't very religious are controlled by the wishes of the genies. You live in harmony with each other."

Apparently, everything I did in my life was the doing of genies inside me because I did not lead a life that was as religious as members of Al-Qaeda.

"It is only the truly faithful like Abbood who suffer the presence of the genies because they fight back and refuse to allow them to take over their bodies," he said. "The truly faithful are in a continuous struggle with the demons inside them. Sometimes genies are tamed and silenced because of the continuous mentioning of God's name, but occasionally, as in Abbood's case, they manage to come to the surface. Genies inside people like you are never angry because they can steer you as they wish without any objections."

****

Two days after the incident in the yard, I was moved to Abbood's cell, which was much more spacious and better ventilated than others. Sunshine penetrated through a hole in the ceiling, and it was much warmer than the cell I had left.

All four residents of the cell were from the south. Besides Abbood from Shabwah, there were Waleed and Jalal Fadhli, the sons of an Al-Qaeda leader from Abyan, and Yafe'I, who came from Al-Yafe'a. Waleed immediately took my mattress and made a bed for me in a corner next to Yafe'i. The Fadhlis and Abbood were on the other side of the cell.

Abbood's father was commander of an army brigade that Abu Basheer had belonged to early in his career. It was out of respect to his former commanding officer that he had moved me here, so I could rid his son of the genie.

Abbood had had a tumultuous life. His father had divorced and abandoned his wife and daughters, whose faces Abbood now could not even remember. He began his career as a soldier in Al-Hudaidah, had worked in the Central Security forces, and took pleasure in beating up peaceful protesters.

Abbood said he had lost interest in beating people up after the experience of crushing the protests in Al-Hudaidah. It wasn't what he was trained to do, he said, and he much preferred being left alone to chew qat all day and night. He was punished for this but couldn't care less. Eventually he had gone AWOL, surviving for months on cakes, candies and soft drinks, while chewing constantly and sleeping only every other day.

"How did you get money for qat?" I asked.

"There's always a way for a uniformed soldier to get money. Stop anyone alone on the street, search him and tell him he is suspected of any violation that comes to mind. Sooner or later, he will empty his pockets to escape."

Eventually the security forces caught up with Abbood, sacked him and denied him a uniform. After that, he moved to Sana'a, where he continued chewing qat and came into contact with Al-Qaeda. I had been told that he had committed murder since he had joined up with them, but figured it was better to go no further with my questions. What I had learned already was quite enough.

Abbood had a stressful family and social history, poor intellect, abnormal behaviour, violent tendencies, a hint of grandiose delusions and a strong belief in magic and genies and was suffering from withdrawal symptoms. I entertained a diagnosis of psychosis and thought antipsychotic medication was worth trying.

I explained this at length to Abu Basheer when I was taken to his office to explain my diagnosis. I said that I thought Abbood was probably suffering from either a personality disorder, for which there was no treatment, or psychosis, for which we could try a course of injections, but I warned him that even with the proper medication it would be at least two months before we noticed any change.

****

Later I asked the two brothers about their detention and they admitted that they had been captured while training with Al-Qaeda. Jalal was 20 years old and a graduate of Aden University Law School; Waleed was 18, had finished 11th grade and wanted to be an engineer. He was very good with his hands and had fashioned a Ludo board and dice from scrap. If the jailers knew about this, he would be put in shackles, so he hid it together with other hard-won tools and handmade treasures in the hole in the ceiling.

While in that cell, I continued my exercise routine of yoga, Pilates and interval training. The two brothers and 23-year-old Yafe'i joined me to prove their athleticism. But as an ex-Special Forces cadet, Abbood was in a class of his own. Despite his affliction, he was fitter than anyone else I had seen in prison.

Chapter 15

Yafe'i told me his life story without holding back. He had started out as a thug earning his living by extorting money, before moving on to Al-Qaeda.

"I always hated Zaydis and wanted to kill them," he said.

To him, 'Zaydis' meant northern tribesman and soldiers, so when he met Al-Qaeda he was impressed with their fellow hatred of Zaydis and their determination to "straighten up the whole world", as he phrased it.

The appeal of Al-Qaeda to young idealists is worth studying. Many young people see things in black and white and strongly disapprove of the corruption they see in the ruling establishment. Consequently, the perceived purity of Al-Qaeda and their associates can be alluring. (I told him, of course, that I thought Al-Qaeda wasn't quite as pure as he thought but had become a tool of the corrupt ruling establishment.)

Yafe'i had divorced his young wife – as far as I could tell for no particular reason – and abandoned his six-year-old daughter. When he talked to our cellmate Waleed, he would address him as "son-in-law" and Yafe'i had promised that he could marry his daughter when she reached nine years old. He wasn't moved by the look of horror on my face when he told me this, firmly believing that girls could marry at that age.

Underage marriage is one of the saddest things that happens in Yemen and is quite common among broken families and the poor. Even establishment clerics defend the practice. As a doctor, I had seen many instances of young girls being taken to the emergency department with torn and bleeding genitalia. Once I had discussed the practice with a magistrate from Sana'a, who had told me that the law did prohibit underage marriage, but that 'underage' meant younger than nine, since this was the age of Ayesha when she was married to the Prophet.

Yafe'i laughed as he told me that he had once earned a living as a teacher of Arabic, despite being illiterate before entering prison, and that he had been hired on merit and not through connections (*wasitah*). I very much doubted him. He also claimed his salary was still being paid to his ex-wife. In fact, he had been taught Quranic recitation (*tajweed*) by fellow Al-Qaeda prisoners and had become so proficient that he himself now taught. His claims made me wonder what political connections he might have.

In the yard, Yafe'i would repeat the same story to jailers: he wasn't a member of Al-Qaeda but a supporter of Herak, the protest movement that advocated secession for the south of Yemen. But he had a very twisted perspective on Yemeni politics, so it was difficult to determine his true connections. He despised National Security forces and the northern tribal groups allied to Saleh and the Islah (Reform) party, but he also respected Houthi leaders despite claiming to be their enemy.

"We, Al-Qaeda, respect Houthis," he said to me once. "We are enemies, but we respect them and they respect us. Both of us are religious and willing to die for a cause, but Islah are not the same. They might be Islamic, but they play politics with Saleh and his allies. Islah are as corrupt as the rest of them, which is why Al-Qaeda has no respect for them."

Yafe'i often bragged about Al-Qaeda's confrontations.

"It is *halal* to kill Yemeni soldiers in uniform," he said. "They act willingly as tools of infidel tyrants and foreigners." He claimed that Al-Qaeda would one day liberate the country and the lands beyond. "We will go on fighting until we control Yemen and will then liberate Makkah. And when we've straightened out the world around us, we will liberate Andalusia."

I think he enjoyed the incredulous look on my face.

"And after that?" I asked.

"London and Washington."

The young man was supremely confident that Al-Qaeda had the upper hand in Yemen. He was also certain that he and his compatriots would soon be set free.

"The authorities can't punish us or execute us because we won't let them get away with it. We've shown them that we'll seek revenge in big ways. National Security has learned the hard way not to torture Al-Qaeda members because there is always payback. We are prisoners of war. Our comrades will kidnap officials and foreigners to exchange for us. It's happened in the past and it will happen again in the future."

Chapter 16

There were three privileges in this cell not extended to other inmates. First, the use of plastic bottles used for sprinkling 'holy water'. Second, a headtorch for use if Abbood's genie rose during the night. Third, a leather restraint that one of the Fadhli boys would use to tie themselves to Abbood every night before they went to sleep, which I considered dangerous as he was so strong.

One day, I asked Abbood if he wanted to get rid of the genie, explaining that he would need months of injections. He was keen and quizzed me about possible side effects. Yafe'i and the Fadhlis were sceptical about what a doctor could do, believing that only experts in the Quran could exorcise the genie that possessed Abbood.

Even if they did not believe I could help him, I still needed their help, as I explained.

"We can give him an injection," I told them. "If it doesn't work, no problem. We can stop it after three months with no harm done."

When I was taken to Abu Basheer to explain my thoughts on Abbood, he maintained a stern expression throughout my diagnosis, before agreeing to follow my suggested course of action.

He then handed me a mobile phone and said: "You can call your family".

At first, I didn't believe it, but he wanted to reward me for my help. However, when I pushed and asked whether they could send me anything, he replied with a stony face: "You can ask them to bring nothing".

It was so emotional to speak to my wife, but I tried not to let it show. I don't like to show emotion, but sometimes I get so overwhelmed that my expression gives me away. Some people think that showing emotion is honest, but I prefer to maintain my reserve.

"How are you?" Salwa asked. I answered "Alhamdu Li Allah" (thank God), which we say in any situation, good or bad, because it is not good to be dismayed by God's will.

I then asked my wife the question that had hung over me since my abduction.

"How did they treat you after they took me away?"

"They were so menacing and kept threatening me the whole time," she answered. "They searched every room and every cupboard, even the ones in the guest room."

"Did they take anything?" I asked, feeling my heart sink.

"They took everything they could. They even stole the housekeeper's savings that she had hidden in her cupboard."

I was crestfallen when she told me that they had taken an antique gun given to my great-grandfather by Sultan Abdul Hamid. It was a masterpiece, and a treasured heirloom. My great-grandfather, Al-Na'eb Mohammad Al-Guneid, was among 40 Yemenis invited by the Ottoman Sultan, Abdul Hamid, to Istanbul, where he was presented with the beautiful pistol, engraved with the sultan's initials. It had been passed down to me and was irreplaceable. No amount of money could compensate for its loss.

Salwa told me that she had moved to Sana'a because Taiz was no longer safe. She had heard from the few neighbours who had remained that there was fighting in the streets and that stray shots might strike our home. The entire city was shelled indiscriminately and snipers were targeting people in the streets.

Hamoud Al-Mikhlafi, the leader of the resistance, had fled to Aden. This news affected me even more deeply than our losses, because it meant that the hope that life would get better was now gone. Hearing the news while sitting in Abu Basheer's office wearing my thin prison clothes, I shivered.

"How is Wigdan?" I asked, enquiring about my eldest daughter in

Florida, who had been expecting her first child.

"She is fine. She gave birth to a boy, who she named Ahmad."

I felt overjoyed. "And how is Mustafa? Has he started school in Canada?"

"Yes, Nagwan is looking after him well. Don't you worry."

Then my son Ahmed came on the line. He raised my spirits by telling me about the outcry from around the world over my detention. I had felt completely forgotten in prison, so it was uplifting to know that this was not in fact the case. He told me he had gone to every official asking for my release.

I knew the call was probably being recorded, but I didn't care. I told him firmly: "Don't you beg or bow to anyone. Do you understand? We bow to no one."

He asked me whether I had received the clothes and cookies they had sent. "No," I replied.

"I took them to the National Security HQ myself. They stole them!" he exclaimed.

I told him not to bother sending anything else, because nothing would be permitted to get to me. Changing the subject, I asked about his baby son, Abdulrahman, my first grandson, who I had yet to meet, and also about my eldest son, Mohammad. Everyone was well, I was assured; I must not worry.

I returned to my cell gladdened by having spoken to them, but depressed and absent-minded. When I told Abbood, Yaf'ei and the two Fadhli brothers I had been allowed to call my family, they were as happy as if it was one of them who had been permitted this privilege. I couldn't tell if they guessed it was a reward for my having offered to treat Abbood.

****

The following evening, a guard came to the door and instructed Abbood to put his hands through the hatch. Before realising what was happening, he was handcuffed and ordered out of the cell. He returned with his feet shackled, complaining loudly that he had been tricked.

Later, Abu Shamekh handed me through the hatch a loaded syringe, with which I injected Abbood despite his initial protests. A calm prevailed inside the cell and Abbood fell asleep. Yafe'i, however, expressed his misgivings, saying that the injection might well provoke the genie.

"Do you want me to show you? Do you want me to provoke Abbood's genie, right now?"

"No, thank you," I said. "It's too early to see the medicine's effects. You can try to provoke the genie a few weeks from now, and then we will know if the medication worked or not."

We slept until the dawn call to prayer. After prayers, the four of them squatted in a circle to recite verses from the Quran by torchlight. Once they finished, we all went back to sleep. Suddenly, a strange, creepy voice came from Abbood's direction.

"Heehee, eeh eeh! O Hakeem! You want to provoke me! Heehee heehee." (*Hakeem*, or 'wise one', is the traditional name for a doctor.) "Oh, senile old Hakeem, I'll show you what'll happen because of this nonsense of yours. You'll pay dearly for what you've done."

The voice was certainly creepy, but I wasn't afraid of the genie – only worried what this ex-Special Forces soldier might do to me if he turned violent. As a result, I showed no sign that I had heard anything, and pretended to be asleep.

A short time later, however, I thought I heard a faint chuckle from Yafe'i and then I heard Abbood go over to him. They whispered for 10 minutes, but I couldn't tell what about. Meanwhile, the brothers seemed to be soundly asleep.

The next morning, a Thursday, passed without mention of the genie or its threats. At lunch, we were served tough meat with the usual potato and rice. The four of them were fasting, as they did every Monday and Thursday, and I wasn't hungry, so I put the food to one side of the room to save for after *maghreb*, the sunset prayer.

Suddenly I was jerked backwards as a towel was put around my neck and someone began throttling me. Instinctively, I put a hand between the towel and my neck and tried to pull it away. The Fadhli boys jumped up and struggled with Abbood, trying to pull him off me. Yafe'i joined them and between them they managed to restrain Abbood, pulling him to the far corner of the cell.

This was the only time in my life when someone actually tried to kill me with his bare hands. I surprised myself that I had managed to stay composed despite the danger to my life. But I quickly told the jailers that I was worried for my life and asked to be moved.

Half an hour later, I was returned to my previous cell with Jamal and Mu'ataz, shaken and hungry. However, it turned out to be lucky that I hadn't eaten that last meal before Abbood's attack, because everyone in the prison who had done so then suffered a bout of diarrhoea and stomach cramps.

Later, Abu Shamekh came to ask my opinion about the sudden bout of illness, and I said I thought it was probably caused by rice being cooked and then left to stand overnight, which had contaminated it. He disagreed – he always liked to dispute my diagnoses.

"No, no – it was caused by a sick, emaciated cow. I saw it myself!"

Yemenis generally have an aversion to consuming meat from a cow and will avoid it in the market, which is why butchers attach an animal's testicles to the carcass as proof that the meat is from a bull or an ox.

Chapter 17

At noon one day, the clang of our iron door being opened startled Jamal, Mu'ataz and me. The commandant stood in the doorway and ordered me to pick up my mattress and blanket and go with him. Beside him stood a Houthi agent.

At the end of the corridor, Abu Basheer ordered me into a nearby cell to wash and told me that I would be released that day.

I was so overjoyed that I could not restrain myself; I hugged him and shook the Houthi's hand. The cell I had been pointed to was cold and dark, so I decided that the outside world could bear me unwashed more than I could bear the cold water. I dressed myself in the only possession I had: a pair of boxer shorts that I had carefully looked after for a special day.

From experience, I learned not to allow myself to get too happy. Sadness and frustration double when one's expectations are not met. So, I started to do what I'm good at: contemplate. I wondered if it was better to be jailed alone or with others. As we grow old, those of us who are in the habit of contemplation like to be left alone from time to time. I was pleased by the novelty of isolation in this new cell.

Moments after the *asr* call to prayer, the cell door opened and another Houthi came in, handcuffed and blindfolded me and took me to another room. When my blindfold was removed, I could see two armed soldiers in uniform in a side room. This was unusual as uniforms were not normally worn at the prison.

One of them walked in slowly, staring at me as if he was hypnotised. I realised that my appearance was eye-catching: I hadn't seen my face in a mirror since my abduction, but I knew that I had become gaunt and emaciated. Stunned at my appearance, he asked me how long I had been there.

"Only sixty-four days," I replied.

Two other men soon entered the room, one of them ordering the guard to unlock my handcuffs and bring the clothes I had been wearing when I had been arrested, my white T-shirt and blue jeans.

The man giving the orders seemed more senior and I guessed he was a *sayyid*. He indicated that I should sit on the bare side of the room while they sat on a sponge mattress across from me. Their mouths were full of qat and the *sayyid* carried a large bag with more inside. He settled himself on the mattress, waved his hands about, rolled his eyes, gave me what he considered a smile and offered the qat to me. When I declined, he insisted that I should partake. I declined again. More hand gestures with the qat and the same non-smile, followed by an insistent "Yes, you should, you certainly should".

"No, thanks. I get nauseous if I chew qat while I'm hungry," I replied politely.

Again, he insisted, so, thinking to myself 'Well, it is not proper in Yemen to turn down an offer of meat and honey at a table, or qat at a *magyal*', I took some and put it down in front of me.

He motioned that I should start chewing, so I put a leaf into my mouth. He stretched out his body, put his hands behind his neck, rolled his eyes and produced a broader smile.

"Oh, you people of Taiz, won't you ever understand and obey the *sayyid*?" he asked.

I shuddered at his words. The way he spoke of his sayyid master, Abdulmalek Al-Houthi, without actually using his name was meant to imply that I and my city should submit to him and his people.

"Impossible," I replied calmly, smiling faintly back at him.

His smile fell and was replaced by a frown as he shouted, "Give back my qat!"

I wondered how I should respond. He thought he was humiliating me by taking back what he had offered me. Etiquette says the opposite, however: returning a gift is an insult, while asking someone to hand it back is shameful. I tossed the qat to him with a scornful grin.

He bent down to retrieve the twigs.

"Back to where you were!" he shouted. "Change into your jail clothes again and go back to your cell!"

I stood up and changed. His companion spoke for the first time, in a nasal Saada accent.

"You'll see! I will visit you at your home in Taiz a year from now. And you will be a good host to me."

I didn't bother looking at him, but I clearly understood the implication of his words. The *sayyid* then ordered me to blindfold myself.

"What is this business of blindfolding?" I asked. "I already know your face, so what difference will it make when I am released?"

"Nothing worries me," he responded. "I've interrogated and put so many people into prison all over Yemen, from Saada to Al-Hudaidah and Sana'a, everywhere."

I was led back to the cold solitary cell in the dim light. Time passed. Or did it? I realised that being alone could be more nerve-racking and, after night had fallen, I began to feel very cold and alone.

All of a sudden, I heard Jamal's screams coming from the end of the corridor. A short while later, a guard with a torch came to take me back to my original cell. Apparently, Jamal had needed to respond to the call of nature, and Mu'ataz couldn't carry him alone, so I was needed. Both of them were overjoyed to see me again.

That was how I spent my 64th day in prison. I didn't know it then, but there were over 200 more to come.

Chapter 18

Late one night there was a bang at the door and I was ordered to pick up my things and move to the next cell, where I was to swap places with Adel, who was better able provide help for Jamal.

Now I was to share with Ibrahim. I had seen him in the yard several times. He always appeared silent and solemn, but nothing is secret in a prison and I had learned a little about him.

Ibrahim was from Al-Bayda and had been captured at the age of 13 with his uncle, who was a member of Al-Qaeda. It was with his more outgoing uncle that the taciturn Ibrahim always sat in the yard.

I got cold vibes from Ibrahim, and it soon became clear why. It was common knowledge that I was the only person in the prison who didn't believe in possession by genies – and this riled him. One day he said to me icily: "So, you say there are no genies, despite it being written in the Quran?"

I tried to explain my views, but he remained disdainful, his comments veering from religion to politics.

"Socialists are atheists and should have no place here in Yemen," he declared.

It was insulting for this uneducated 16-year-old to subject a doctor 50 years his senior to an inquisition, but soon our conversations were reduced to a minimum. Instead, Ibrahim spent his time busying himself beside the corner tap, washing, praying, reciting from the Quran, chanting poetry and singing religious songs. While doing all this, he tried his best to direct waves of scorn and hatred at me.

Ibrahim was much stronger than me, so once again I had to consider the possibility that I would face another violent attack. To take my mind off things, I amused myself by returning to scenes from *The War of the Roses*.

The bigoted attitude of Al-Qaeda inmates was the cause of some of the greatest distress in the prison. For example, one inmate was badly beaten by an Al-Qaeda prisoner because he didn't perform extra prayers in addition to the five daily ones. I myself was scolded countless times for all sorts of things, such as using my left hand for food when a proper Muslim should only ever use his right. I just couldn't stand people telling me what to do. On another occasion, when asking a Salafi prisoner for something, I began my request with *"wahayatak"* – an affectionate, colloquial form of 'please'. "Don't say that – it is *haram!*" he snapped.

Ibrahim and I would perform the five prescribed prayers together, but there was tension even in this. Ibrahim knew that I liked to start my prayer immediately after the prayer call (*athan*), but he would continue his recitations and rituals while I waited impatiently for him to end.

"Don't you know that you can do all the extras after the *farida* [main prayer]?" I protested.

He ignored me, so at the next prayer time, immediately after *athan*, I jumped up and prayed alone. The next time, he joined me without delay.

Like all pious prisoners, Ibrahim fasted on Mondays and Thursdays. Because I did not, I would keep his food aside for him to eat after the *maghreb* prayer. Since he was always nagging me during mealtimes, I asked to be served food on my own plate and to eat alone. The cook frowned but was sympathetic and, without a word, gave me a separate plate.

In this way, I passed four unpleasant days sharing a cell with Ibrahim – a boy who was in his third year of incarceration. Despite the disparity in the time we had served, however, I was becoming an authority on prison life. Although no relationship lasted indefinitely, in the case of Ibrahim it was shorter than most. Nonetheless, I managed to endure his silent hatred for a whole week.

Things changed one day when a third inmate was thrown into our tiny cell, which was barely big enough for two. As the newcomer, Omar, squeezed his mattress between mine and the wall around the washing corner, he told us he had smuggled a Saudi Arabian dissident into Yemen. The Saudi had tweeted against the Al-Saud royal family and was trying to flee the country and get a Yemeni passport. He had paid Omar 50,000 Saudi riyals, but they had both been arrested by the Houthis when they went to pick up the new document.

Omar had been smart enough to leave his earnings behind in Saudi Arabia, but their captors had seized whatever they could from the two men before handing them in at National Security headquarters, where they were beaten and interrogated.

After we had exchanged stories, our conversation paused and Omar quietly sang what I thought was a northern tribal *zamel*. Ibrahim immediately smiled and went over to sit beside Omar to join in. I was surprised, as he had never before shown any sign of curiosity about another person. I could only surmise that they were singing an Al-Qaeda poem that shared the ups and downs of a tribal *zamel*. When Omar told Ibrahim what he planned to do when he eventually got out of prison, Ibrahim's excitement soared.

Before Omar went to Saudi Arabia, he had studied at the Salafi Institute in Dammaj, where he met the love of his life, the daughter of a German who was also studying there. They both got on so well with Omar that they promised to arrange a visa for him to enter Germany. He was planning to use the money he left behind in Saudi Arabia to start a new life there.

Ibrahim was fascinated, and bombarded Omar with questions, wanting to know how he had managed to attract the attentions of the German woman. He was becoming very possessive of his new friend, while I was quietly listening to the story and enjoying the change from the unpleasant atmosphere of the previous few days.

We heard that in Sana'a, where he and the Saudi dissident were living in Omar's family home, there was no electricity, so he used some of his earnings from smuggling to buy a solar panel. Omar said he wasn't with Al-Qaeda, just an ordinary Salafi who wanted to live like any other person – to marry and start a new life.

The ideologies of Salafism and Al-Qaeda are similar except for one thing: Al-Qaeda believes in violence while Salafis believe in *Wali Al Amr*, that is, obeying the rightful ruler. Both, however, reject Yemen's multiparty system.

Omar began talking about ISIS's gains in Syria and Iraq, saying to me: "ISIS will prevail in Islam's victory around the world, won't they, Doctor?"

When I disagreed, he asked me why.

"No single group can be victorious over the entire world," I said.

"But we can only win by Islam, isn't that true?"

"We can only win through education, scientific learning and hard work," I said, but I could see he wasn't convinced.

Omar slept a lot and wasn't bothered when food arrived. He would reluctantly wake up and eat a little, and then go back to sleep. Ibrahim pestered him to eat, pray and, above all, talk with him, but mostly in vain. Had it been anyone else, this would have been cause for an argument and perhaps even a fight.

During the few hours Omar was awake, he would ask me about current affairs and history, much to Ibrahim's annoyance. Omar was quite interested in my explanations, but Ibrahim behaved as if he disapproved of Omar seeking opinions of a secular person such as me. Over time, Ibrahim softened after he came to the decision that he did want to know what I thought his future held.

"Your problem is that eyes all over the world are on people like you," I told him. "The authorities are wary of releasing Al-Qaeda prisoners because they fear you'll return to violence after your release." But I didn't want Ibrahim to lose hope, so I added: "If your family can provide guarantees that you'll behave well in the future, then you might be released."

On one occasion, Omar amused us by recalling his experience inside a Saudi jail, where he had been sent for hitting two young Saudis who had insulted him because he was Yemeni. Each prisoner had his own cell with a fridge, a television on the wall and a remote control. He said the food was very good and there was always more than enough to eat. Fruit and soft drinks were on the house. Pocket money was given to all inmates and those with special privileges were allowed to buy foodstuffs at the little prison shop and cook for themselves. He joked that, when his release date arrived, he hadn't wanted to leave and the jailers had to drag him out three days later.

****

Five days after Omar's arrival in our cell, the door was opened and I was ordered to pick up my bedding and get out.

"Why are you leaving us, Doctor?" asked Omar, as if I had a choice in the matter.

It was around 2:00 in the morning as I gathered my things, wondering where and why I was being moved.

"Do you know English?" the guard asked me as we walked along the corridor. I guessed that I was being moved to an American inmate's cell by orders from higher up.

I was right and was soon shoved into the cell of 'Al-Amriki'.

"What the … what's going on?" he exclaimed.

"I'm your new companion," I answered in English, trying to spread out my bedding. It was inky dark in the cell and we couldn't see each other's face.

"Oh … good," he said.

It was the first time he'd had a cellmate, and he had one who could speak English.

"I'm Abdulkader, from Taiz. I'm a prisoner of conscience, jailed for things I wrote."

"I'm Mark from Tennessee," he replied.

He told me that he had eaten nothing in the two weeks since he had been arrested, surviving on water and tea. I realised that they had put me in with him hoping that if Al-Amriki had an English-speaking companion he might give up his hunger strike. I had a few precious dates hidden about me, which I offered to him. He politely took one and we bonded immediately. I was relieved to be away from the suffocating presence of my Salafi and Al-Qaeda cellmates, and Mark was pleased to have someone to talk to.

I insisted that he should eat more, but after three large dates he said he had had enough. Instead we talked – a lot.

"I was just praying to Jesus for a sign that there's a light at the end of the tunnel. And you came in – you're the sign," he said.

I was pleased that in these spartan surroundings I had been upgraded to being a sign from Jesus.

Mark and I fell asleep around dawn, waking hours later with the arrival of Abu Basheer. He asked what Mark wanted to eat. I interpreted for him: fish, fruit and boiled eggs. Normally, our captors would not have cared less if anyone went on hunger strike and died, but they did in the case of Mark, who thought he had been granted a special diet because he was stubborn and serious in his strike. I, on the other hand, thought he was given this diet because he was American; but I subsequently came to believe that it was to appease him because of the fate of a companion who had been arrested with him, about which I learnt later.

For a few days, the jailors were very generous. Some of the meals were better than Christmas feasts for Mark and Eid meals for me. He always insisted that we share. Some days, we didn't even bother with the usual jail fare we were given alongside the fish and fruit, though the guards were careful to collect the remaining fish bones, which they said we might use as weapons or to commit suicide.

"Don't worry," I assured the guard. "I think both of us would like to have many lives – neither of us are thinking of suicide."

****

"Christianity is all about sharing," Mark often said.

"Islam, too," I said, wishing to stress that our religions were similar. "The Prophet Mohammed said, 'You are responsible for your seventh neighbour'. They should not be hungry while you are full."

He told me that Christians prayed before eating, then shared, so this is what he and I did. And he appreciated my respect for his prayers, especially when I added an 'amen' to what he'd prayed.

I asked Mark if we could share some of the fruit with Jamal, who I explained was paralysed and, I knew, loved fruit. Being a devout Christian, Mark agreed and also began praying for Jamal before each meal.

Mark had come to Yemen as a construction expert to supervise repairs to the Sana'a Sheraton Hotel, which was leased by the US Embassy for USD1 million a year as part of its plan to create a 'green zone' in the manner of Baghdad. It had been out of business since a new Mövenpick Hotel had been built nearby, so the Kuwaiti owner was delighted to rent his property to the embassy.

Mark had been arrested by Houthis at Sana'a airport together with his companion, an ex-marine called John Hamen, the head of security at the Sheraton. They were both accused of being spies when they returned to the country after a trip to Djibouti. They were subsequently brought to the jail, where they were immediately separated, never to see each other again.

"I think the decision to arrest you was made when you were still in Djibouti," I said. "Their intention was to extort money from your government."

Mark admitted that he hated the Houthis but felt guilty about his feelings since he believed Christians should not hate.

"I can't understand how an armed nation like yours allows Houthis to control you!" he complained.

He thought that Houthis were foreign invaders, so didn't quite understand the situation. I tried to explain by analogy.

"Imagine that in a twist of fate the Ku Klux Klan took the upper hand in the US. Then try to imagine that a strong foreign country supported their agenda. The KKK members and the leaders of the foreign country believed that they were a superior race, entitled to rule. If you can imagine that, then you can see how the Houthis, like the ayatollahs of Iran, claim they are descendants of the Prophet and thus 'entitled' to be the masters, using arms to carry out their agenda."

I still wasn't sure he had understood, continually asking why he had been put in "this lousy jail" and assuring me he wasn't a CIA spy.

Once he told me that the first thing he had asked after his arrival was which way was east, because he believed that's where Jesus Christ would be resurrected when the time came.

"But you're already in the east," I told him. "You can face anywhere when you pray.".

He also proudly told me that he went to church three times a week, drove the church bus, taught bible classes to kids and gave a tenth of his income to the church.

"From your net income or after tax?" I asked.

"I asked our priest about that," Mark replied. "He told me that if I wanted God's complete blessings to my prayers, then I should donate ten percent net, and if I was happy for partial blessings, I should make my donation after tax. So, I give ten percent net."

"What does your wife say about your donations to the church?"

"Oh, she doesn't like it. She thinks our family needs the money more than the church," he said.

"My agreement and sympathy are with your wife," I replied.

He also told me he thought there was a reason for everything and the reason he had been arrested was to make him think how he could better serve Jesus. He had vowed to visit every home in his neighbourhood when he got back to the US, preaching the gospel. If he succeeded in bringing just one person to the church that would be enough, he believed.

I didn't say a word. It is nobody's business to comment on another person's religious convictions. I didn't like it when Salafis did it to me and I would be a hypocrite if I did it to Mark. However, I did think what he believed about fate and destiny was not much different from what I had heard some Sunni inmates say, or what our Shia jailers said during interrogation.

I wanted to hear from him what was happening beyond the prison walls, but he did not appear to know much about events in Yemen or the political reaction in the region. Instead, I asked him about a topic I was interested in: whether Hillary Clinton had won the Democratic Party nomination for the forthcoming US election.

"Not yet. She will, but she will lose the general election. She ain't good", Mark said.

"Why? I think she's one of the smartest politicians in the US, and certainly smarter than her husband."

"She's no good, she is a liberal. Liberals don't pray," he said.

I had learned from experience that it is most unwise to antagonise a pious man by discussing religion, especially in a cramped prison cell. I wanted to remain on good terms with Mark – and also to remain in his cell, where I was getting much better treatment.

Changing the subject with a laugh, I told Mark that I had read a newspaper article saying that Trump might win the Republican nomination.

"No, he won't – he ain't religious either. Trump is a liberal like Hillary and the Democrats. Liberals believe in evolution – I don't. God created everything in one go."

Mark asked me one day if I would like him to send me a copy of the King James Bible when we were released

"Would you read it?" he enquired. "When I was in Afghanistan, I gave a Bible to a Muslim co-worker, and he liked it."

"Gladly," I answered.

Now and then I told Mark Islamic versions of Biblical stories, including that the most cherished woman in Islam is Miriam (Mary), the mother of Isa (Jesus), who has a complete surah dedicated to her in the most eloquent and beautiful prose.

"Look, we're Jews, we're Christians, we're Muslims," I said. "Religion is our speciality and trade in this land. We're the ones who gave religion to the world. It took us three thousand years to come up with Judaism, four centuries to develop Christianity and only two decades for Islam. As we moved forward passing from one faith to another, it required less time because each one learned from its predecessor. For example, Muslims share with early Christians the practice of ritual washing before prayers."

When we came to a discussion of Armageddon and the Day of Judgement at the end of the world, Mark said that he believed "what is written by the Baptist Elders".

"Do you mean elders living now?" I asked.

"Yes, they write regularly about the latest prophecies and truths revealed to them by God," he answered, promising to send me copies when we were released. I was intrigued to learn what elderly 'wise men' from Tennessee were still writing.

According to the simplified version Mark shared with me, their prophecy was that, on doomsday, Jesus would side with Americans in a battle against the evil Antichrist, who would side with the Russians, Chinese, Iranians and Germans. Jesus and the Americans would prevail and then everyone would become a Christian before the end of the world.

Strangely enough, Salafi Muslims believe something similar: the resurrection of Al-Maseeh (the Messiah) before the battle against Al-Masekh Al-Dajjal (the Antichrist), although it is not mentioned in the Quran or the Hadith (the sayings of Prophet Mohammed). The concept of the Antichrist was introduced after Mohammed's lifetime and the foundation of Islam. Nevertheless, many Muslims accept it without question.

The only difference in the Muslim version of the story from Mark's is that the Messiah will be a Muslim and, at the end of days, everyone in the world will become a Muslim rather than a Christian. I appreciated that, as a courtesy to me, Mark didn't mention Jews or the fate of Arabs and Muslims in his retelling, sparing us the wrath of the faithful.

When Biblical themes were exhausted, I would try and entertain

Mark with other stories, which he enjoyed listening to like a child at bedtime. Many of my tales related obliquely to evolution.

"I love your stories, Doctor," he said with a smile after one such. "I love very much the way you tell them. But I don't believe in them, or in evolution."

I tried to take a more subtle approach with one of my favourite stories. This time he listened with interest and amusement. I began by describing my second year of medical school at Ain Shams University in Cairo, where I had a physiology professor who was teaching about physical reflexes, such as sneezing and coughing. He told us that there was a neurological pathway for everything and challenged us to suggest a phenomenon for which there was no scientific explanation.

I wanted to ask about yawning but didn't dare to in case I lost face in front of my classmates. Instead, it took three decades for me to learn the answer to my unspoken question, which I eventually found in the *British Medical Journal*. The article explained yawning in the context of packs of animals led by the alpha males of the group. Apparently, there are two characteristics in their yawn: to denote tiredness, and to act as an 'infectious' reaction in large groups. As the weakest members of a pack tire early, they will yawn and this will spread through the pack until it reaches the leader. The alpha will then feel tired and signal the pack to rest. Yawning is not a reflex like sneezing, but a communication signal that developed through social evolution.

Mark liked this and gave a faint smile and nod. I had mentioned the troublesome word 'evolution' and he had not reacted negatively!

****

Many years earlier, I had come to the conclusion that people fought for three reasons: money, power and the desire to spread their seed. Faith, ideology, race, colour and every other cause of conflict were merely the icing on the cake.

The worst examples of human conflict, such as in Sarajevo and Rwanda, happened because of the inability of people to share limited resources in a common territory. In both those conflicts, rival groups fought each because of sectarian and ethnic identities, but the conflicts were more about land and resources. Christians fought Muslims and Hutus fought Tutsis in order to remove the 'other'. But whenever there is difficulty sharing limited resources among people of similar identities, some zealous ideologue comes up with the way to split them apart.

I tried to explain my thoughts to Mark, who listened politely.

"For me, things happen because they were meant to happen by the will of God – not by evolution or chance," he countered.

Mark was a true-blooded religious Christian American, but in this way he was similar to the Salafis of Yemen. They do not accept explanations based on learning and knowledge either, preferring instead to follow a tradition of beliefs derived from religious faith.

****

In his life back in Tennessee, Mark had three overriding passions: religion, his wife Crystal and Fox News, in that order.

After one interrogation, Mark returned to the cell clutching a photo of him with Crystal. National Security officers had hacked into his laptop and when they found the image of him and his wife had printed a copy for him, which he stuck to the cell wall next to his mattress.

I came to learn that Mark was a combination of kindness and raw physical power and had a tendency to turn angry and throw a tantrum. But during our early days together, he was generally in a good mood.

I knew how fond he was of his wife, so would sometimes ask: "What would Crystal be doing right now?"

Mark would carefully work out the time difference before responding.

"Let's see, it's now eleven o'clock in the morning in Tennessee, so she would be on the porch having a cigarette break."

He did not approve of his wife's bad habit and when I told him that my wife Salwa also smoked, we laughed. He hadn't imagined that we would share the same problem. It brought us together and made us closer buddies.

Chapter 19

Mark not only started to eat but, when he saw me exercising, he joined in.

I could see he had been in good shape before his hunger strike and knew that he was conscious of the importance of a healthy diet and moderate portions, as did I. The only difference in our eating habits was that he ate quickly and liked to chat over meals, whereas I ate slowly and preferred not to talk. Even when we were only being given the standard prison food of bread and beans and maybe a little rice and meat, we were determined to keep up with our exercises. Despite this, we became thinner by the day and our beards grew long and ragged.

Mark was curious about our National Security jailers but couldn't quite grasp the difference between those working for Saleh and those working for the Houthis. The striking contrast between Abu Basheer and Abu Shamekh, however, made it easier to explain.

Abu Basheer, the commandant, was a pro-Saleh National Security professional who represented what was left of the old state. He remained reserved, but it was he who had arranged for our temporary special diet. I was to develop a respectful, if not cordial, relationship with him after I went to advise him about some severe medical problems he had as a result of a festering gunshot wound in his leg.

In fact, my medical care of the commandant continued even after I left the prison and was in Cairo awaiting a Canadian visa. Abu Basheer managed to track me down on WhatsApp and I helped arrange for him to be operated upon by a well-known Egyptian orthopaedic surgeon who was a specialist in infected bone fractures. It was a complete success and the commandant was profusely grateful for my help, but I declined to renew our acquaintanceship.

By contrast, Abu Shamekh, the top Houthi man, was a bombastic, rude, crude loud-mouth. Even so, I developed a working relationship with the man because he appreciated my willingness to act as the prison's unofficial doctor.

Mark despised Abu Shamekh's shouting and always wanted to know what he had said. I did my best to diminish the insults with incomplete translations and did the same whenever Abu Shamekh asked me to translate what Mark had said.

My general aim was to keep the peace and avoid conflict but sometimes, when Abu Shamekh was particularly vindictive, I scolded him.

"Look, I don't translate everything you say to Mark, nor do I tell you what he thinks about you," I said. "If I translated what you both say to each other, he would go on another hunger strike."

"That's exactly what a good mediator should do," he replied with a smile after a short pause for thought.

I hadn't realised until then that mediation had been added to my medical duties. Over time, however, it was the latter that earned greater privileges, especially as I continued to offer advice to Abu Basheer about his leg wound. Months later I was in his private office to advise him on his medical treatment. As I started examining a simple x-ray of his leg against the ceiling light, a sudden very loud explosion deafened us, and I felt the floor beneath us rise and fall.

"An air strike!" Abu Basheer said. "The security brigade, I'm sure it hit our security brigade!"

The commandant rose quickly and left the room to investigate, followed by a guard. Inmates knew about the presence of the top-secret brigade that guarded the prison with 200 men. They acted as if they were part of a large training camp, with fake morning drills and the like to fool outsiders.

Left alone in the room, I felt pleased knowing that the site was under attack. This was the second occasion that a Saudi aircraft had struck the location where I was being held. Despite the danger, I wanted my captors punished for what they were doing to the country. I wanted the entire Saleh-Houthi nightmare to end.

****

In our three weeks as cellmates, Mark and I had not been allowed in the yard. Mark was used to working outdoors and was finding it extremely difficult to remain inside all the time. I told him I thought we might finally be allowed out that week but, though he was pleased to hear this, he was a little worried about coming face to face with Al-Qaeda prisoners. I tried to put his mind at ease, assuring him that I would look after him.

The next Tuesday, a shout went along the corridor to get ourselves ready for the yard and, as before, we were led from our cell in the same humiliating manner, barefoot, blindfolded and chained. Mark wore a T-shirt and jeans and I was clad in my blue prison overalls. We were lined up with other chained prisoners in the corridor, where the guards threatened us not to speak for what seemed a long time. Finally, we were led slowly to the prison door, and shuffled into the yard after stumbling down the cinder block stairs.

There was a tangible air of excitement, as everyone wanted to know about the foreigner. I did my best to introduce Mark in the best light: Yes, he was American, but he was a very religious man who said his prayers every day. I was also whispering into his ear, describing who was and who was not Al-Qaeda.

A few Al-Qaeda prisoners objected to him just because he was from a sect that followed John the Baptist, until one of their leaders, Zarqawi, pacified them.

"Yahya was good and is mentioned in the Quran," he said, "though of course he shouldn't have a religious following of his own."

He then told me I should try and convert Mark to Islam.

"You'll be lucky if he doesn't convert me to Christianity first!" I shot back.

Zarqawi was shocked and not at all amused. He acknowledged Mark's piety, but nonetheless wanted to straighten up his thinking.

"You should adopt Islam," he said to Mark, asking me to translate his words.

"Leave him alone!" I snapped again.

"Maybe the best thing is that we kidnap the American to teach him about Islam. And we will kidnap you with him, Doctor, so you can do the translation," growled Zarqawi.

The thought of being kidnapped and becoming a prisoner of Al-Qaeda after being abducted by Houthis was too much to contemplate. I don't know how my expression changed as I shuddered at the thought, but I remember the look of astonishment on Zarqawi's face. In his mind, there was no need for me to be upset because he was only having a casual chat about how best to straighten out Mark as part of Al-Qaeda's overall agenda of doing the same to the world as a whole.

Once we returned to our cell, I washed myself while I was still warm from the sun.

"Those Al-Qaeda inmates were okay," said Mark from his corner.

He appeared to be thrilled by his first encounter with members of the infamous group.

****

Soon after this incident I was allowed to make another call to my wife, three months after the first. This time I called from a room where others were permitted the same courtesy. It was packed, so everyone could hear each other's private thoughts and messages. To my initial disappointment, my call failed to go through, but then I calmed myself because I did not want my emotions to be public knowledge. And in any case, the next day I was allowed to try again, this time on my own, and got through to my son Ahmad, who told me that Salwa and Mohammad had moved to a flat owned by my wife's uncle.

On this occasion I was allowed to ask my family to bring me some supplies. I requested the best olive oil for Jamal, the best *hareesah* for

Yafe'i and the Fadhlis, and the best honey for Mark. I also asked for 50,000 rials because I dreaded the possibility of being thrown out of jail in the middle of night in the middle of nowhere with nothing on me.

For myself, I asked Ahmad to ask Salwa to make me some 'naughty' cookies stuffed with dates and nutmeg. I was generally strict about eating healthy food; 'naughty' things were the occasional treats she would bake for me. I also asked for nuts, raisins and dark chocolate, and socks, vests and trousers because it was so cold in the cell.

Ahmed updated me on the situation in Taiz, which made me very depressed. The city had become the front line of the conflict, our neighbourhood was in ruins and intruders had ransacked our house, stealing many of our possessions.

****

Two days later, Abu Basheer and Abu Shamekh came to our cell together – to make sure there was one Saleh supporter and one Houthi – with two cartons of clothes and goodies. They searched every single item, every plastic bag, every nut and raisin and told me that the receipt of all of these goods was a special privilege shown to me. They also said that the pistachios in the package were normally forbidden because of their hard shells, but they would turn a blind eye this time.

I was thrilled by the packages, which reminded me of care parcels my parents used to send in my childhood when I was studying in Cairo in the 1950s. But I didn't want to be bothered with keeping everything in order, so I gave much of it away. The warm clothes made a great difference to life inside the cell, yet I didn't have the heart to wear the clothes while others could not, so each time we went to the yard I would go barefoot and in Guantanamo-style overalls like everyone else.

I gave Mark honey and he very much enjoyed the homemade cookies. They became a regular part of our breakfast – one each day for 55 days. He included my wife in his breakfast prayers until the cookies were finished. I smiled to myself about the strictness of his thanksgiving – cookies gone from the table, Salwa gone from his prayers – though he did ask me several times for the recipe and planned to ask his wife to make some when he returned to Tennessee.

It took me two weeks to hand out my gifts to my friends because I had to be careful who to ask to take them. I sometimes offered gifts to the guards as well. I even offered something to Abu Shamekh and Abu Basheer.

"I would never eat something from you!" the former exclaimed. "There will never be salt and bread between us."

Abu Basheer's response was more nuanced.

"Personally, I would be happy to eat with you, but I don't want to set a poor example to the guards. We tell them not to accept anything from prisoners."

****

One morning we were surprised to be taken to the yard uncuffed and without blindfolds – a rare treat, especially as we had only been outside the day before. This time we were sharing the yard with inmates from the second floor of the jail, who were normally kept apart from us.

An audible murmur greeted us as we stepped into the sunshine. I returned the welcome of these inmates with a wave and a shout of "*al-salam tahiyyah*" (peace is my greeting), a common way to greet a crowd en masse.

I knew a few of these prisoners from my medical rounds, but most were new to me. I couldn't avoid noticing that the atmosphere was untypically relaxed; there was a buzz of conversation and even Abu Basheer was smiling.

He pulled out his mobile phone and spoke into it – making sure that I was within earshot – checking to see that fish and qat had been bought. Others who had also overheard looked at me quizzically, especially since northerners were notoriously averse to fish.

I maintained a poker face but whispered to Mark: "We're going to be having fish for lunch today".

He asked me how I could possibly know that. I shushed him and said

I would explain later.

But a fish lunch we did have, relishing every mouthful, even though it was a little overcooked. We ate everything – head, fins, tail, burnt parts – except for the 'dangerous' bones, which were duly collected after we had finished our meal.

This was also the first time I met the famous interpreter of dreams and Al-Qaeda chief, Tareq Al-Ma'eili, though I didn't know it at the time. To me he was just a tall, dignified fellow inmate who had asked me for some medical advice.

****

I later found out why we were allowed this extra ration of fresh air: Mark was soon to be visited by Derhem, Abu Basheer's boss from National Security headquarters, and our jailers wanted him to say that he was being well treated.

The visit from the National Security bigwig took place a few days later. Mark was taken from the cell and, half an hour later, the door opened and I was summoned out, handcuffed and marched off to the administration office, where I was plonked into a chair beside Mark's, facing this man who all the guards feared.

"Hah! They tell me you're a terrorist," Derhem said, trying to intimidate me.

"That's a new one!" I said with a grin.

"How long have you been here for? Do you still remember any medicine?"

I didn't respond.

He gestured at Mark and asked me: "Is he a spy?"

"No. He couldn't be. He's just a simple construction supervisor. And anyway, he's a Salafist."

My defence of Mark startled Derhem, especially my description of him as a Christian version of a Salafist.

"What about his employers, the American company?" asked Derhem.

I told him what Mark had told me, that his bosses were ex-US military, that he was just refurbishing the hotel, and that the US Embassy was renting it from its Kuwaiti owner and planned to make a few bucks after withdrawing their staff from Yemen by subletting the building to the UN.

When we were sent back to the cell, Mark told me that Derhem had taken his photo. Later, I heard from the commandant that Derhem had gone straight from the prison to the airport and flown abroad.

The following day, Mark was taken and grilled by his usual Houthi interrogators. They were upset by Derhem's visit; it was none of his business to question the American, they said. And they were even more disgruntled when they heard he had photographed Mark. They considered Mark to be their prisoner and clearly wanted to profit from his ransom themselves. For his part, Mark was riled that they persisted in calling him a spy – despite me trying to reassure him that it was all about money.

****

Mark was usually kind, soft-spoken and exceedingly polite. But he sometimes lost his temper, which frightened me. He had the biggest biceps I had ever seen, and I didn't want him to use them on me.

"Look, Mark, we are both depressed and angry. Being vocal will only make it worse. Making angry gestures will make it worse. We really should keep calm inside this cell," I suggested.

Sometimes I succeeded and everything went well; at others the atmosphere soured and we didn't talk for days.

"We should translate our anger into thinking of ways to expose their evil when we get out," I said.

Most of the time he agreed, but he occasionally directed his anger at me, which made me cross. I would then ignore him until he had offer me a heartfelt apology, which I would readily accept.

"Thank you for forgiving me," he would say. "You'd be a good Christian. We believe in forgiveness."

But his moods became more frequent and more expressive.

"There is a limit to forgiveness," I warned him one day. "You can't have all these tantrums and expect instant forgiveness every time. Even your wife wouldn't take it."

One of his habits during our time together was to drum on the walls and ceiling, trying to get messages to the man he'd been arrested with, John Hamen. Mark said that his rhythmic drumming was 'red Indian' and would only be understood by a fellow American. Occasionally, we would hear an answering drumbeat.

"That's him," Mark said knowingly.

However, we never saw another westerner in the yard, except George the Hungarian, nor did anyone I questioned know anything about another American prisoner. In particular, I took great care to quiz the second-floor prisoners about his whereabouts during the unscheduled trip to the yard. They said that there were definitely no Americans on their floor.

Even so, when I had received my parcels, I sent a little of everything as a present to John, the American I had never met. When I had asked a guard to relay my gift, he had looked curious and hesitant, but quietly nodded his head in agreement and silently took my present through the hatch.

On Christmas Eve, I sent John Hamen another present with a different guard. He made the same hesitant response and quietly took it away. Mark demanded of the guards that he wanted to pray with his fellow American on Christmas Day, but they refused.

Eventually I found out why the guards had been so shifty, when one day Adel, the best source of gossip in the prison, sidled up to me in the yard.

"We heard through the pipes that he was 'found' dead in his cell, a few days after he arrived," he whispered. "Those in the neighbouring cells heard the rush of guards, and when they came out of the cell, they were carrying a figure wrapped in a blanket."

"That can't be true!" I exclaimed. "I sent him a present at Christmas and the guard took it for me."

I didn't have the heart to tell Mark about Adel's gossip, so, since I was his only source of news, he did not get to learn about the fate of his friend until after his release. But I knew from Mark that John Hamen had seven children waiting for him at home in Florida.

Chapter 20

The next time I was in the yard, Adel came up to me again.

"Sheikh Tareq Al-Ma'eili sends his greetings and thanks to you," he whispered.

"Sheikh Tareq who? And he thanks me for what?" I asked.

"You examined Sheikh Tareq when you were here with the second-floor inmates," he explained.

Adel had heard of my meeting with the sheikh via the pipes and now that he had explained matters to me, I realised who he meant.

"Aah! So, the tall man I examined was the famous Tareq!" I exclaimed.

Tareq Al-Ma'eili was renowned for his leadership of Al-Qaeda's attack on government troops on the Abyan coast under the command of General Somali, a Saleh loyalist. His night raid killed 200 soldiers without loss, after which he and his men had escaped to Marib.

He had been arrested in Sana'a at a much later date, after he came to the capital in disguise seeking treatment for gunshot wounds. Tareq had once issued a *fatwa* saying it was acceptable to waste water in the jail if it was considered necessary – even though it is usually forbidden by Hadith to waste any water.

"Because communication between inmates is necessary, wasting water in the lavatory is acceptable," was his explanation.

When I had shared a cell with Jamal, Tareq had always sent me his regards after interpreting Jamal's dreams over the water switchboard. As Makkah always appeared in Jamal's dreams, Tareq's interpretations were always favourable, cheering Jamal for days on end.

****

On another occasion in the courtyard, the tall, imposing figure of George the Hungarian – chained to his cellmate, Afraim – entertained us with anecdotes about himself. Speaking in classical Arabic with just a hint of a tribal accent, George told us that he owned a public bathhouse in Al-Bayda, near Marib. One day a tribesman asked George to play some music while he used the facilities, so he put on a recording of a symphony. But soon after the music began, the tribesman stormed out.

"What's this? I asked for a song!" he demanded angrily.

He seemed not to care much for the classical music that George favoured.

I already knew that George was musical. From my cell I had once heard from afar the unexpected sound of a rich baritone singing arias. Having learned that it was him, I asked him to sing again in the yard, but he declined, pointing to his throat. On other occasions, he did sing beautifully for me, mesmerising me with his voice and theatrical delivery. However, I seemed to be the only one to appreciate his voice and often had to shush others around us.

I was intrigued by George and learned by chatting to him in the yard that he had a fascination with nomadic Bedouins. He believed that the only remaining true nomads in the world were in Yemen's south and the Sahara Desert south of Algeria. His mother shared his passion and had devoted herself to a study of the nomads of the Sahara.

By profession, George was a sound engineer and had spent the preceding four years in Abyan and Shabwa recording Bedouin music. He had also composed operas, which were performed by singers he had trained in Aden. He was deeply worried about losing the recordings, which were all on his laptop – now in the hands of the Houthis – and would raise the topic whenever he had the ear of a sympathetic jailer.

Unfortunately, there didn't seem to be anybody negotiating for George's release, and he had all but given up hope. He asked me to try to get in contact with his mother when I was released through a Facebook account he had in the name of Che Guevara (*that* name again, I thought!). However, when I did eventually get out, I couldn't find the account, try as I might, and felt very bad about not fulfilling my promise.

George once explained that he had converted to Islam after discovering that his grandfather had been a Muslim, which inspired him to find out more about the religion for himself, studying in a mosque in Hungary and learning to read the Quran.

One day, I unintentionally spoke to Kemo – another nickname, derived from his given Arabic name of Abdulhakim – in English, at which he told me that he only spoke Arabic. I later found out that George had good English, German and French besides his mother tongue.

He walked around openly clutching a miniature Quran and was proud of his deep knowledge, often winning Quranic arguments with Salafi or Al-Qaeda prisoners. He also told me that he had read and memorised Hitler's *Mein Kampf* in German, perhaps one of the few people in the world equally well-versed in these two books in their native languages.

****

The fish meal we enjoyed after our visit to the yard with the second-floor inmates was one of the last times I was to break bread with Mark. Soon I was transferred to my 13th cell, a crowded six-person chamber mostly full of Al-Qaeda members.

When I first got there, George was inside, sharing a joke with Omar, the man who had been arrested trying to procure a passport. George and I were swapping places, so he was taken up the corridor to move in with Mark.

I knew everyone in the new cell from the yard or from my medical rounds. I was given a cordial welcome and they arranged my sleeping space for me.

As well as Omar – who promptly went to sleep – another of my new companions was Otmi, an Al-Qaeda man from Otmah, with whom I discussed the genuineness of the Yemeni version of the organisation. He listened without interruption to my assertions that it was a handmade version, born and nurtured by Saleh. At first, he said this was not the case, but he was eventually won over by my arguments.

"You are educated and know better, Doctor," he said. "All I want is to go back home – to my village in Otmah. I would even avoid going to Dhamar [the governorate's capital], where people believe they are a superior class to us. They are as racist as the Houthis. I just want to settle down, get married and live peacefully attending to our farm." As a promise to himself, he then muttered: "Islam has a God to take care and protect".

In any case, I was not to be in that cell for long. For some reason that I never found out, the jail administrators thought it was not good for me to be in a cell full of Al-Qaeda, so they moved me again to one where there were no members, although all its occupants had been accused of being so when they were arrested.

Chapter 21

In terms of inmates, my 14th cell was the strangest of all. Its five occupants had all lived in Sana'a and three had known each other since childhood. All of them, though, had one common denominator: they had been implicated in some way by a man called Faghi, who was also now an inmate.

My new companions were Ali Dasmi; his neighbour, a van driver called Jareed; Lieutenant Al-Zoughli; and the two Daki brothers whose family was originally from Taiz governorate.

I knew Faghi – his nickname, meaning 'open-mouth' – from the yard, where he had been boasting of having been called a prince of Al-Qaeda by the interrogators. He wasn't, but he seemed to enjoy the upgrade in his status. I remember him trying to be friendly with the lieutenant, who clearly did not want anything to do with the man who had sold him out.

My cellmates told me that Faghi was a small-time villain and conman who earned his living by extortion. He would send anonymous threats to Isma'ili merchants in the name of Al-Qaeda despite having no connections to them. They usually paid up without informing the police.

He was certainly imaginative in his schemes. One story I heard was that he would lure young would-be Al-Qaeda members and, for a fee, send them off to 'training' in Hadhramaut, despite having no affiliation himself, which is why he was so amused at being called a 'prince of Al-Qaeda'.

When he was arrested by National Security officers, he was severely beaten.

"With every slap on his face, he gave up one of our names," alleged Al-Zoughli.

The older Daki brother agreed.

"The last time I saw Faghi was two years ago," he said, "but nevertheless he gave my name to spare himself an additional slap."

All my new cellmates had been arrested because of Faghi's false testimony of their membership of Al-Qaeda. Indeed, many young men were arrested because of their bearded appearance and strict piety and subsequently became more sympathetic to Al-Qaeda after being erroneously labelled as such by the authorities.

The irony of my cellmates' situation is that before their arrests none of them had been very religious. In fact, they did much that was forbidden, yet now had become much more observant, praying and reciting the Quran regularly. But they hated Al-Qaeda with a passion.

Ali Dasmi and the younger Daki enjoyed a set routine every evening. Ali Dasmi was illiterate but wanted to recite the complete Quran so he persuaded the young Daki to read a few suras each evening, which Dasmi would repeat, poorly at first, leaving Daki to continually correct him until he got it right. Dasmi's motivation was to ease his misery; Daki's was to earn his God-given reward. But sometimes his actual reward was somewhat unexpected.

"Ugh ... how dare you fart while we're reading the Quran!" he would shout when this happened.

Dasmi would always deny it and they would squabble until Dasmi would laugh and say: "I didn't mean to!"

"No, you did it on purpose!" Daki would counter, until the smell would waft over to us and then dissipate, after which the good-natured boy would return to giving his lessons while Dasmi's friends either ignored the incident or admonished him, depending on their mood.

This episode brought to mind a scene from Cervantes' *Don Quixote* in which the servant, Sancho Panza, is occupied with a call of nature while his high-minded master is totally absorbed in knightly matters. I couldn't resist laughing, but it ceased to be funny when the stink reached my corner.

On average, humans pass wind 14 times a day. Multiplied by six people – and given our daily diet of beans and bread – this gives some idea of the atmosphere in the cramped, unventilated space. Life in jail was difficult anyway, but to my mind the accumulated emissions were akin to a global extinction event of the sort that ended the dinosaurs. I laughed at the thought of my new cell contributing to global warming, thinking to myself: "Well, if I don't become extinct at the hand of the Houthis, maybe I'll end as the dinosaurs did".

I wasn't eating much in those days, but still insisted on being served on my own plate, as I had been doing since sharing a cell with the teenager Ibrahim. When the cooks appeared at the door, my cellmates would hand my plate through the hatch saying, "This is for the Doctor," and then pass the single plate for the other five of them.

I would eat only two or three flatbreads a day, whereas they were always hungry and would gratefully divide any food I hadn't eaten between them after dawn prayers. But because I wasn't eating much, my ribs, hip bones and cheek bones were becoming more prominent as I lost weight. I tried to force myself to eat whatever rice I was given and could usually manage this when it was hot, so I ate as soon as it arrived.

To pass the time, Dasmi told me about some of the misfortunes that had befallen him thanks to Faghi. On one occasion, Faghi had sent him to Hadhramaut with instructions to contact certain Al-Qaeda members when he got there.

"Suddenly my senses and mind returned to me, and I was disgusted with him and myself," claimed Dasmi. "I was also terrified, so I managed to sneak away from them and returned back home to Sana'a the following day."

I told him I didn't believe his story. Who would travel more than a thousand kilometres for no sensible reason?

"That's me. I sometimes do things impulsively," he said, matter-of-factly.

"Why were you arrested this time?" I asked.

His story was that Faghi had been plotting to kidnap a child of a prominent merchant and had recruited Dasmi and his friend Al-Zoughli – who were always in need of petty cash to support their qat and alcohol habits – to carry out the task. They had hired Jareed and his van to study the boy's routine as he went to and from school, but when a bunch of tribesmen became involved in the scheme, Dasmi and Al-Zoughli said they wanted out.

"We didn't like their faces. They looked sinister, and this made us uncomfortable, so we abandoned the plot," he explained.

On other occasions both men hid Faghi from the authorities, since, as Al-Zoughli said, "we played together as children so we couldn't turn him down when he needed help".

However, after his arrest, Faghi had given up his former friends' names and they all ended up in jail. They were disgusted with him and now considered him the lowest possible kind of man.

"We would never have done the same to him," Al-Zoughli and Dasmi agreed.

They felt very aggrieved. Not only had a crime not been carried out, as just discussed, but National Security should not have been involved.

"Even if there was cause to make arrests, we should have been arrested by ordinary detectives and tried properly in a court. This is not the job of National Security," opined the lieutenant.

As mentioned, their time in prison was making the men more pious, except for Dasmi, who kept a sly smile on his face as he watched his friends perform their rituals.

"At home, I wasn't keen on praying and never read the Quran," Al-Zoughli confessed, "but now I vow to never drink again and to stop touching women."

"The first thing I'll do when I get home is have a drink under the stars on the roof of my house," Dasmi said defiantly.

"Don't say that! God is listening to you! You'll not see any good when you say such things," his compatriots exclaimed.

"God knows me and knows that I'm good. I know you all too well, so please spare me your hypocrisy and preaching," Dasmi retorted.

They kept their mouths shut, wondering about his daring. We come from a culture that never dares to turn down a preacher, even one who is not well known.

"I never touched a woman besides my wife," Dasmi continued. "I love my wife and my daughters and never had any business with other women. My only business with other women is with the woman I buy *khamr baladi* [homemade alcohol] from. I don't have a taste for smuggled foreign drinks – they are far too expensive."

He told us his drinking stories, saying that mainly he would just enjoy drinking alone on his roof. But on some evenings with us he almost cried out of longing for a drink.

"You know you can have your drink here inside this very cell," I casually said to him one day.

The five turned towards me, eyes popping out of their heads.

"How?" Dasmi asked eagerly.

"When Mu'ataz the Syrian was in the Al-Qaeda cell, he saw them make a brew from dates, even though they were devout. They said it was *halal* if it was fermented only for three days."

I then delved into the science and offered them information about which they had no clue. Nevertheless, they listened with interest as I explained the chemical processes of photosynthesis and fermentation, carbohydrates, by-products and so on. When I had finished confounding them with my scientific explanations, Dasmi implored me just to tell him how he could have his drink.

"We have yeast in the soft parts of our kudam bread. You can taste it – it is that faint sour taste. That's what is needed for the fermentation. All we need now is sugar. I will gladly give you one of my plastic bottles and you can make your own alcohol."

Since sharing a cell with Mark, who had bottled water brought to him from outside, I was one of the few prisoners who had access to plastic bottles, and I took great care of them.

"I know how to get sugar!" announced Dasmi. "I'll claim I am sick and tell the cook that my blood sugar is low and I will faint if I don't get some extra sugar."

As the result of a great deal of wheedling, he succeeded, after which he excitedly asked for further instructions.

"Put some sugar in the bottle and half fill it with water, to give space for the gas released by fermentation," I explained. "Then you can add some rice and potatoes along with bread; they're carbohydrates, too. Then add some of your tea for colouring. Close the bottle tight to allow the yeast in the bread to start the fermentation and wait for three days."

"Doctor! This is *haram* – you're reducing your and his chances of being blessed," warned the others, apart from the older Daki brother.

"That's not true – it's *halal* if fermented for only three days. Besides, I know the Hanafi sect allows wine."

Daki senior had apparently digested my science lecture.

"Can we do the same with honey?" he asked.

"Yes, of course."

"I have a gallon of the best Yemeni honey," he said – much to the bemusement of his more pious younger brother.

Three days later, Dasmi excitedly asked: "Doctor, can I open the bottle now?"

"Yes – but be careful! Press on the bottle lid firmly as you open it, or it will shoot off and your drink will spill."

He did as instructed, but the drink still fizzed up, and Dasmi jumped towards the drain, licking the bottle as he tried to save every drop. Then he took a huge gulp and looked at me, his eyes full of joy.

"Well? How is it? Is it close?" I asked.

"*Mazaj!*" he happily exclaimed, meaning it met his expectations. "Same smell, same taste, and I wouldn't mind if it didn't turn my head the same," he said as he started to dance. He was a great dancer and his happiness made him look like Anthony Quinn in the movie *Zorba the Greek*.

Days later, Ali Dasmi finally got to the end of the Quran, having repeated word-for-word after Daki, and I congratulated him profusely.

"The credit should go to Daki first," I added. "He put up with you and endured this tedious routine night after night for a whole month. He certainly will get his reward from God."

Dasmi asked Daki to start again from the beginning. They did, and we had to endure their noise once more.

****

Al-Zoughli was in his mid-20s and from the Bilad Arrous tribe, neighbours of Saleh's Sanhan tribe near Sana'a. He adored Saleh and named his only son, Affash, after Saleh's family name.

As soon as I was moved into their cell, Dasmi wanted to tell me about his friend's status, explaining that his brother was a senior officer and aide to Al-Za'eem. He addressed his friend as 'Al-Afandem', a traditional honorific of senior Ottoman commanders. I simply called him by his first name, Ali – which was alright by him.

Al-Zoughli was a talented folk poet. I thought one of his compositions, in which he begged his eldest brother to work for his release, particularly good. Another poem, in which he implored his brother to help him after a previous arrest, was so good that it had his brother rushing to his assistance.

Apparently, Al-Zoughli's mother was now cross with the elder brother, the brigadier, for not helping his little brother in his current difficulty. Dasmi confirmed this

"Al-Afandem could be released in no time, but his brother wants to teach him a lesson," he said.

"I swear to God not to drink or do anything forbidden from now on," Al-Zoughli pledged many times.

Redemption was important for Al-Zoughli and he awoke before dawn every day to read the Quran. Soon he would be joined by Jareed and the younger Daki, who would read together until the dawn prayer call. After prayers, they would loudly recite a part of the Quran (*mu`awwathat*) to keep bad spirits away. Al-Qaeda prisoners from the neighbouring cell would bang on the walls in protest, accusing them of *bida'ah* (a religious innovation that was beyond pure Islam), for which they would go to hell. My cellmates took this personally and would raise their voices even more, and when the two groups met in the yard, they would squabble over their differing practices.

Al-Zoughli loathed Houthis and believed that Saleh would return to power and finish them off.

"The Houthis' strength is being eroded by the day," he explained to me. "They are zealots and ideologues, and their best fighters are being killed at the fronts. A time will come when they will be helpless and then President Saleh will finish them."

"Are you sure?" I replied. "I think the Houthis have penetrated Saleh's establishment. When they joined the Sana'a protests, they attracted Hashemites like a magnet. I also know that Hashemites living among the tribes around Sana'a joined the Houthis in Change Square [a protest camp set up in Tahrir Square]. Also, all the Hashemite officers are loyal to the Houthis, and I've no doubt where they will be on the big day. I know that Houthis have exploited their ability to move freely among the tribes to win them over and use whatever bondage that was still around from the old days between the northern *sayyids* and tribesmen."

Most Yemenis believed that, in the end, Houthi and Saleh would clash with each other.

"Besides," I continued, "Hezbollah in Lebanon and Qassem Soleimani in Iran are keeping a close eye on the Houthis. They have decades of experience in intrigue and fighting all over the region. They have won all their wars and will lend their experience to the Houthis until they dominate all of Yemen."

Al-Zoughli dismissed my arguments.

"That's nothing," he said. "Didn't you see the huge crowds that turn up whenever Al-Za'eem asks them to come?"

"But they came for cash handouts and because of pressure from sheikhs and landlords," I replied.

"Look, Doctor," countered Al-Zoughli, shaking his head. "Al-Za'eem ordered half the Republican Guards to stay at home, so just wait until they are called back. Al-Za'eem has left running the state to Houthis and if those Republican Guards don't receive their salaries they will rise up and overthrow them. The tribes around Sana'a would join in, too."

He told me that some retired officers and sheikhs around the capital received up to a million rials from Saleh.

"Saleh will never be let down by the Sana'a tribes," he assured me.

Dasmi agreed with his friend, illustrating the point by telling me about his uncle, a Saleh loyalist called General Al-Hadidi, from the Bani Matar tribe.

"Good grief, is he your relative?" I exclaimed. "I read an English article just before my arrest saying that he received forty million US dollars from Saudi Arabia to keep Hadhramaut safe from Al-Qaeda."

Dasmi smiled mischievously. It is a matter of special pride when a Yemeni tribesman earns money from all sides in a conflict, especially when the Saudis are involved.

"Mind you, I think Saleh's troops in Hadhramaut facilitated the Al-Qaeda jailbreak – all Al-Qaeda stunts are staged by Saleh to lure the Americans into his plans," I said.

I asked Al-Zoughli if he was wary of Houthis winning the hearts and minds of the people, now that they ran neighbourhoods.

"On the contrary," he said. "The Houthis tried to fool people that they were idealists, but actually they are as corrupt as we are, if not worse. At least we did it subtly and with style. They do it with a roughness and crudeness and our bet is that people will get sick of them and revolt. Don't worry, Doctor, the Houthis will be finished off by Saleh."

Al-Zoughli thought that I only wanted Houthis to go away and would be pleased by his last statement. When I explained otherwise, he was shocked.

"Doctor, do you support Ali Mohsen?"

"What good did General Mohsen do for me or the country to deserve my support?" I replied. "I actually chewed qat with Saleh, but I've never even met Mohsen."

"Mohsen is gone! The Houthis will be gone!" said Al-Zoughli. "And we will return. Al-Za'eem is no longer interested, but his son Ahmad Ali Saleh will become the president of Yemen."

"But what about the National Dialogue Conference and the new constitution?" I retorted, starting to get angry.

"You're dreaming, Doctor. No one talks about such things any more. You're out of touch. You have been in jail too long. We have an army that has gained experience and is full of experts." He also had no doubt that Saudi Arabia would be defeated. "The Saudis have no boots on the ground, and they will never have," he said. "If they try, they'll be no match for us."

We argued for hours, but his confidence couldn't be shaken. However, through our discussions, I came to learn much more about him.

****

Al-Zoughli had joined the Republican Guards when he finished sixth grade, still little more than a child, but he was accepted thanks to his brother's influence and his tribal background. He enjoyed being financially independent at a young age, progressed well, and soon became an officer, at which point his brother arranged a scholarship to a Russian military training centre near the Chinese border.

"Every year, I was top of my class in the academy and graduated as number one," he bragged. "I spent the best four years of my life in Russia. I rented an apartment downtown near the academy and gave spare keys to several girls, filled up the fridge and shelves with food and bottles. I sneaked out from the academy every night to party, and then would creep back into my dorm at first light."

I doubted his tales – after all, Russians are not stupid, and he would hardly have been top of his class if he had behaved in such a way. But he insisted this was true, and some other stories were even wilder. The other cellmates just listened with envy, while I didn't believe a word.

I thought to myself, "Think twice before arguing with a Yemeni, thrice before arguing with a tribesman and much more before arguing with a soldier".

With all our arguments, Al-Zoughli and I gradually became cold towards each other and we ended up barely speaking.

Chapter 22

Dasmi and Jareed were neighbours in the old quarter of Sana'a and often went together to wedding parties at which famous wedding singer Al-Ta'efi performed. They were close and loyal friends but were different in so many ways.

Jareed had a beautiful voice and sang a lot of very pleasant folk songs. When he hadn't sung for a day or two, I would ask him to sing for me, which he would often do, especially if he was grateful for medical advice or treatment that I had given him. But at other times he ignored me and looked the other way.

Al-Ta'efi was Jareed's favourite singer. He sang old songs and wrote his own compositions using everyday colloquialisms. There was something charming about them. But Dasmi strongly disapproved of his friend's idol because of his personal habits and lack of integrity. It became quite a bone of contention between them.

"What do you think about this, Doctor?" Jareed asked me one day. "I always argue with Dasmi that the singer's personal habits and ethics are his own business. We should judge the singer by his songs, not by his personal faults."

"This is a difficult question," I replied. "My answer is that arts are arts, and personal liberties, even if one does not approve of them, are a different issue, so we shouldn't judge one by the other. My only reservation would be if the personal liberties included taking advantage of the weak, children or women. In these situations, it is a crime and not just a different, peculiar, perverted or disgusting habit. But at the same time, Dasmi has every right to be disgusted."

Jareed lived with his parents and family in Sana'a. When his father finally gave up hope that he would continue his education, find a job or start a business for himself, he bought his son a minibus to earn his living transporting people. Jareed's father was a military pilot who had been trained in Russia.

"My father flew regularly to Moscow in the past," Jareed recalled. "He always brought us nice presents when he returned."

Jareed was a tall, slim, young man who grew a moustache and beard and had shaved his head. He had a habit of staring at you, or at whatever he was doing, with such concentration that he would make you feel uncomfortable. He never smiled but sometimes, in response to something that only he found funny, he would burst into laughter. He could be mean, too. He was especially insulting towards the older Daki brother, on whose behalf I intervened several times to rescue him from Jareed's vindictiveness.

The younger Daki brother was possibly the strongest person in the cell. Most of the time he watched in silence, but when he thought that Jareed had overstepped the mark he exploded angrily in support of his sibling. Jareed would behave himself for a few days after Daki junior's intervention (or mine), but he always returned to his ways and started picking on the older brother once again. It was one of these unexplainable things between people; sometimes one person can be nasty to another for no logical reason.

Jareed also had strong convictions, and no reasoning could make him change his mind. One day he told us that his grandfather was "still strong and full of zest because growing up he ate *samn baladi* [butter from cow's milk] daily".

Many Yemenis say the same thing, but it was not true – there simply weren't enough cows in the country. There is an old saying that villagers in Yemen's hill country would shout to passers-by in the wadis: "Come and have lunch with us. It's Thursday and we have *samn*".

I explained to Jareed that, historically speaking, the people had a poor diet, which is why they were always thin.

"Look at pictures of people from a few decades ago," I said. "They were very thin and short, which means they were calorie- and protein-deficient."

"Not true," he snapped angrily at me. "People in olden times ate and drank *samn* every day, all the time."

I realised that when Jareed's mind was set no one could budge him. He told us how he disliked discussing politics with passengers in his taxi. As a supporter of Saleh, he especially disliked the opinions of Islah supporters.

"Many passengers talked about politics freely, even Islah supporters. But I told them to either shut up or get out of my van," he said.

Despite being pro-Saleh, Jareed was not quite as supportive of the ex-president as Al-Zoughli was. On several occasions when Al-Zoughli exaggerated the merits of Saleh, both Jareed and Dasmi argued with him, saying they didn't think he was honest but, even so, they supported him against both Houthis and Islah.

"Look, I pushed people in the *souq* to go to Saleh's sit-in at Al-Tahrir Square," Dasmi told Al-Zoughli. "I was always there, supporting Saleh." He turned his face towards me with a mischievous smile, before adding: "Yes, we all went for the two thousand rials and the free lunch, but although Saleh was bad, we also wanted him to beat Islah."

Jareed shared the same point of view: Saleh was bad but Al-Ahmar and Mohsen were worse. Both Jareed and Dasmi were keen to call themselves neutrals. They saw all politicians, parties and religious movements as corrupt and having ulterior motives, often saying: "They're all bad: Saleh, Mohsen, Hamid, Houthi, Muslim Brothers, Islah, Salafists, Socialists and Nationalists".

Al-Zoughli also felt that they were all bad – with the exception, of course, of Saleh.

"I'm willing to sacrifice my life for Al-Za'eem," he said on one occasion.

Many politicians and highly educated people, a chunk of the so-called intellectuals, share Jareed's and Dasmi's views, while claiming neutrality in the same way. I agreed with them that all politicians have bad records historically and ulterior motives for the future.

I told my cellmates that all Yemenis were on a dangerous path, suffering chaos and turmoil until we 'all' agreed on following the new constitution based on the National Dialogue Conference. The problem was that both Saleh and the Houthis had their own independent armed forces, and they believed that the new era would not provide them with enough parliamentary seats to rule the country. The size of their constituencies did not provide them with power comparable to their armed forces or ambition, so they bonded together, despite their animosity, creating the military coup that ended the consensual transition process.

"I cannot be neutral between the Saleh-Houthi coup and those who opposed it," I said. "Anyone who claims 'neutrality' between a strong, armed side and an unarmed side is not neutral. Practically speaking, they are siding with the armed side. If both the stronger and the weaker side are bad, that is another matter and should be tackled separately based upon the National Dialogue and the new constitution, under which the 'goodies' and 'baddies' are treated equally under the law," I concluded.

****

The Daki family was originally from Taiz governorate, though the boys' entire lives had been spent in Sana'a, where their father rented a house with a gate and yard – all of which sounded very impressive to the others in the cell, who lived in the crowded old city. The boys both got as far as secondary school, but then lost interest in education.

All five cellmates exchanged vows that they would keep in touch after they got out of jail. They anticipated being released as one package, since they had in common the fact that their arrests were all based on Faghi's false accusations. The younger Daki promised to host a lunch and qat session in their yard.

"I know it is very un-Yemeni to chew qat in the open air, but it will feel so good after this suffocating cell," he said.

Dasmi vowed to be generous, too.

"Well, I will slaughter a sheep and invite you all for a traditional lunch," he offered. "I'll bring Ta'efi the singer for you, and I'll invite you for qat the whole afternoon and evening."

"Would you come, Doctor?" Dasmi asked me, as if my acceptance was not to be taken for granted like the others. I felt mischievous and started to impose outrageous conditions on my attendance, to all of which he readily agreed.

The older Daki said that his wife was an excellent cook, describing at length the menu that they would have in his apartment. He promised to invite all of us together with our wives – who would, of course, dine in a separate room. There followed an argument about whose banquet would be better, which nearly came to blows before I tried to calm things down.

"Stop it! If you carry on like this, you won't be friends when you are released. Besides, you'll end up broke if you carry out all of your promises!"

The elder Daki always sought to impress Al-Zoughli, an arch-supporter of Saleh. In particular, he was keen to talk about his actions during the anti-Saleh protests in Change Square, claiming he had founded the White Shirts Movement (moles who had infiltrated and disrupted the protests). This was a common tactic of all the reactionary, pro-regime groups to undermine the progressive groups, including the women's movement, liberals and socialists.

I simmered silently as I listened to Daki telling his version of events. We are a country that is going through hard times. We have ambitions and aspirations to join modern times. But those ambitions are constantly undermined by that sort of behaviour.

Daki also liked to brag about his connections with Saleh's relatives.

"Al-Aqwa'a, Saleh's brother-in-law, often sought my advice, and he has chewed qat in my apartment," he once told us. "The two of us discussed things together for hours. And Tawfeeq Saleh [the ex-president's nephew] liked me very much. He offered me a good job, but

I turned it down. I have greater ambitions and ideas."

He was eventually persuaded to tell us about his great idea. He claimed to have invented a blend of spices that when added to sandwiches made them irresistible. The blend was a secret and he vowed he would never divulge it to anyone.

Al-Zoughli offered to sell his car in order to buy Daki a mobile kiosk from which to sell his 'irresistible' sandwiches in a 50–50 partnership. Dasmi jumped at the deal, saying he would guarantee a spot in the Bab *Shou'oub souq* that would ensure their business was a hit. In every cell I have been in, everyone had a dream of a business that could not fail.

I also got to learn how the brothers came to be in prison. Two years earlier, Daki senior had been attacked by Houthi militia while working as a cigarette distributor. He lost his stock and his truck to them and was severely injured. As a result, his father had to use all he owned to bail his son out. Daki wanted revenge against the Houthis, which eventually led to him coming into contact with Faghi. When Daki eventually refused to follow through with his hare-brained kidnap plot, the course of events that led to his arrest had been set in motion, with Faghi subsequently giving him away to the security forces.

Daki junior was unlucky to get caught up in his brother's fate. When security forces went to arrest the elder brother for the botched kidnapping plot, they found young Daki – who used to work at Al-Bank Al-Dawli – in his brother's apartment and arrested him too.

"They're holding me here in this lousy jail for only thinking about a plan that was never carried out," said Daki senior, close to tears.

Hearing the sorry story, Jareed began teasing him and, when his brother and friends didn't intervene, I shouted at him to stop.

It was peaceful for a few days and Daki expressed his gratitude to me for standing up for him against Jareed. I told Dasmi, who always listened with respect to what I said, that he should help control Jareed's behaviour.

****

Being kidnapped was horrible. The conditions in the jail were horrible. The jailers were horrible. But as usual, my fellow inmates were even worse.

I spent two months in that cell, during which time I resisted the intense desire for fresh air and sun because I could no longer bear the painful ordeal of going to the yard handcuffed and blindfolded. Right from the beginning, I had resented being bound, but my eagerness for fresh air and sunshine had made me put up with it. Initially, I was also curious and wanted to know everything about the jail, the jailers and the inmates.

Prisoners knew the design of the jail by heart. They could tell the number and size of cells, steps, stairs and the tiles in every corridor. Nevertheless, the jailers blindfolded us so we would not know the place. Everything was supposed to be top secret.

What's more, the jailers were temperamental. Sometimes they allowed us to chat in the yard and, on some occasions, encouraged those who could sing to entertain the rest of us. I couldn't believe how much I enjoyed listening to a song in the sun. But frequently, the jailers did not want to hear a peep and returned anyone who talked to his cell.

The pleasure of sun and fresh air no longer compensated for the humiliation of being chained and blindfolded and the capriciousness of the guards. For four months, I didn't go outside at all, preferring to stay alone in my cell, even at the risk of my health. After months of this, a jailer came to me and asked why I didn't go outside. I evaded the question and asked if I could be moved to another cell because the current one was overcrowded and stuffy.

A few days later, the jailer asked me to grab my things and get out. I needed the change and was pleased. Six people with different habits, different manners and different ways of reading the holy book at odd times, crammed back-to-back in a dim, narrow, airless and humid cell was torture.

When I finally left the cell, I said to my cellmates: "I leave you with a *wasiyah*" (a request or wish).

They eagerly asked me: "What? what?"

As I stepped out of the cell, I turned to them and said: "Jareed, you must stop bullying Daki".

Jareed nodded in agreement and I said goodbye.

Chapter 23

Before I left them, there had been a brief period when another inmate had been billeted in our already crowded cell: a millionaire currency-exchange owner from the capital, who had been in custody for just two days. The clean-shaven and cheerful man arrived wearing a fresh, well-ironed *thobe* but without a mattress or blanket.

Upon learning his name – Al-Toro – my companions showed him the utmost deference. Daki senior immediately jumped up to give the newcomer his mattress and squeezed himself between his brother and Al-Zoughli. All five stared at him as if they could not believe their good fortune to have such a man sharing the cell.

Al-Toro asked everyone's name and hometown and my cellmates formed a semicircle around him and questioned him about life outside. I stayed in my place. I was not as awed as they were by the distinguished newcomer in the shining white, neatly-ironed thobe.

He told us the rial was spiralling downwards and all currency exchanges had been ordered not to sell dollars. He described how he had been arrested.

"National Security men bugged my phone and overheard the details of a deal to sell a large amount of dollars," he recounted. "Usually, I'm careful and never discuss business over the phone, but this was such a good deal that I couldn't turn it down – and my client was important, too."

I wondered about the kind of person who had enough rials to buy dollars from Al-Toro at the implied higher price. I also wondered where he got his dollars from and what he would have done with the proceeds from the deal. After all, who would want to keep stacks of devaluing currency in his safe? Of course, I kept these questions to myself.

We already knew that, several days earlier, Saleh had summoned his followers to Sab'een Square, so Al-Zoughli was keen to know how the rally had gone. Al-Toro gave a dramatic expression and waved his arms about to express the huge size of the crowds – streets were packed with people cheering for Al-Za'eem in defiance of the Saudis.

"At the end of his speech, Al-Za'eem told the crowds to attend a Houthi rally later in the afternoon in Al-Jiraf [the Houthis' stronghold north of Sana'a]," Al-Toro told us.

The size of Saleh's crowd pleased my companions but depressed me, though I tried not to show it. To them, it proved that Saleh still had the upper hand. They thought that, if Saleh prevailed, they would soon be released and their chances of economic advancement would strengthen.

I felt isolated, alone in my corner, as I heard the others discuss the news. I quietly asked Al-Toro if I could put three questions. He nodded.

"What's the source of foreign currency in Yemen?" I asked.

"From expatriates and immigrants abroad," he said.

"Is this enough to pay for the goods that my friends here are telling me flood Sana'a's malls?"

"No. Money from expatriates doesn't cover the cost of imports. It's too little."

"Okay, so where does the foreign currency needed for imports come from?"

"This country has been blessed with honourable businessmen who pay for Yemeni imports in euros and dollars. They had the foresight to transfer their deposits to New York and Paris, and they pay from there."

I could not comprehend why any businessman, good or bad, would give up his foreign currency in exchange for the collapsing Yemeni rial. Those who need rials would eventually spend them on the war, I thought. Who would finance Yemen's war by importing goods from abroad with hard currency and then selling the products for rials inside the country? Who would supply Saleh or the Houthis with oil from abroad, which was then sold to the people at black market prices?

"I see that Taizis are very clever and good businessmen," Al-Toro commented, looking at me with interest.

Later, when I started to exercise, he was surprised. I explained to him the merits of physical activity and invited him to join me, which he did.

"Thank you," he said afterwards. "I feel like I have a new body. I got rid of my aches, too."

Before dawn prayer the next day, a soldier opened the hatch and handed us a mound of fresh bread that had been specially baked for the soldiers together with a large dish of yogurt, onion, tomatoes and cucumber. Everyone woke up at once and ate with gusto – the other five hadn't had food like this since their arrest.

"You should have been arrested earlier," I joked to Al-Toro.

Everyone laughed but didn't stop munching. This treatment was clearly for him, and we were happy to benefit from his presence.

Late that afternoon, Al-Toro was taken away. As usual, the one who gets released left without a word or even a wave of his hand.

Chapter 24

In my eighth month of imprisonment, I was moved into my 15th cell, and what a pleasant change that was – just one cellmate and fewer noxious fumes!

The cell was very narrow, with room for only two mattresses in an L-shaped arrangement around the washing corner. However, the air was unusually stagnant as I recalled from my medical rounds, though, to mitigate this, the door-hatch was kept open all night. This illusion of freedom seemed like a luxury.

I was welcomed into my new quarters by Menbehi, a stocky man who I had treated some months before for a fungal infection between his toes. Since this often goes hand-in-hand with diabetes, I had lobbied for him to be tested for this. He was grateful for my care, so gave me a warm welcome.

Menbehi was from Saada. He was an unusual man who did not hesitate to tell me all sorts of wild stories about his adventures, starting off by explaining why he shouldn't be in prison.

"I've already spent time in the Central Security jail for smuggling hashish to Saudi Arabia. I was pardoned after five years in jail and went back home to Saada," he said. "I own two houses in good locations in Sana'a and had already made enough money from selling hash and decided to take no more risks. I also have a big farm on the Red Sea and do good business importing goods from Dubai. For that reason, I have no more use for hashish. It is my nephew's fault that I'm in jail this time."

I asked him about his hash business and he explained how the drug is brought by sea from Pakistan and then smuggled from the south coast until it reached him. He would then arrange for it to be transported into Saudi Arabia.

"Yemenis prefer qat and possibly alcohol, and have not developed a taste for hashish," he told me.

So, I asked, if he had already been released from one jail, how did he come to be in this one?

"National Security officers stormed my house looking for my nephew. He had some hash on him and told them that I knew nothing about it – which was true – but I was still arrested and brought here with him," Menbehi said.

I asked whether his nephew's stash was for sale or for personal use.

"It was a whole block. More than for personal use," he said, cursing his nephew who was being kept away from him in a separate cell.

I asked if he smoked hash.

"Look, Doctor, a little hashish and alcohol before sex make it wonderful!" he said, educating me in the manner of a man full of wisdom about the facts of life. "I always ate meat at mealtimes and chewed the best qat while running my business. But at night I gave my attention to other things. The best things in life are business and women. On trips to Dubai, I made money like no one else, and I could have as many women as I wanted. I enjoy both."

Menbehi had many interesting tales to tell and wasn't at all shy about sharing them. Earlier in his life, he had earned a living by transporting foreigners from the Saudi border to the Salafi Religious Institute in Dammaj. He claimed that he was just a truck driver in those years and his passengers included Europeans and Americans.

"My first passenger was a European. He accidentally left his bag in my truck, so on my return a few days later, I brought it back to him. He spread the word and told his Salafi contacts on the Saudi side that I was a trustworthy driver who could take them to Dammaj. Honesty is good for business," Menbehi said proudly.

"How many westerners come to Dammaj to study Salafism?" I asked.

"Quite a few."

The Dammaj Institute had no precedent in our cultural heritage and contradicted Yemenis' temperament. Its curriculum was based on Wahhabi doctrine from Saudi Arabia, which is alien to Yemenis, whether members of our Sunni Shafi'i sect or of the semi-Shia sect of the Zaydis. It was founded in the early 1980s with Gulf oil money to teach Salafism to Yemenis, Arab foreigners and westerners. But in late 2013 it was closed after being stormed by the Houthis with the tacit approval of the Gulf and Western countries.

In prison, Menbehi used to suffer bouts of impatience, anger and sadness but was generally quiet and composed.

"Doctor, what do the Houthis want from me?" he asked once when he felt particularly overwhelmed by his imprisonment.

"They want your money," I suggested. "They've guessed that you have a fortune, but they don't know where it is."

He accepted my reasoning without admitting anything.

"They will get nothing," he said firmly. "I hinted to my interrogator that I would give him something if he got me released and he seemed to pay attention for a few sessions, but then I never saw him again."

Each day Menbehi tested my memory about the phone number of a well-connected sheikh he had given me.

"The sheikh is shrewd and he knows what makes the Houthis tick. He will find a way to get me out. In anticipation of a day like that, I let him live in my best house in Sana'a without paying rent," he explained.

"Why doesn't the sheikh get you out now?" I asked.

"I'm sure that he doesn't know I'm here, otherwise he would have," said Menbehi, as if he needed to reassure himself. He was confident of his investment in the sheikh, but also expressed anger towards his two sons, who were looking after his farm, suggesting that they hadn't yet contacted the sheikh. He then got me to memorise their number and promise to call them when I got out and tell them to call the sheikh.

Menbehi was another one who enjoyed joining me in my exercise routine.

"This is the first time in my life that I have exercised. You're very useful, Doctor," he said gratefully. "One can benefit from you. All the others here in jail just like to talk nonsense and I have never benefited from any of them."

Despite his fearsome appearance, life was much easier with Menbehi than in my previous cells, which had usually been full of meddlesome, pious cellmates. But after two weeks, he was abruptly moved elsewhere. I felt sad. He was one of the few cellmates who minded his own business and never imposed himself on me. There were subjects of conversation in which he had no match, yet he also knew his limitations and didn't hesitate to ask questions to expand his knowledge.

****

Stories by inmates about their abilities to charm women, whether a shepherd girl or a city girl, were endless.

For example, one cellmate told me how, if he could attract the attention of a young girl, he was satisfied with nothing more than a glance, a smile or a short chat. His neighbour on the next mattress reprimanded him for such unseemly behaviour. Soon another cellmate, who was very pious and recited the Quran all the time, couldn't resist the temptation to brag. He said that, when it came to charming girls, he was the best. It sounded ironic coming from a man who was supposed to be pious, yet he couldn't resist boasting about his abilities. For no reason, he dared me – who was only listening and not participating in the conversation – to do better than him if we happened to compete for the attention of any girl. He told us stories about charming four girls who later became his wives.

Stories like this could go on for days and my cellmates eventually insisted that I tell stories about the women I had met. I just smiled and changed the subject. I never tell such stories. I cherish memories of every girlfriend I've had throughout my life and would never disrespect them by describing our encounters. These women visited me quite often in my jailhouse reveries. They were very helpful in jail – it was amazing how clearly I could hear their voices from more than 50 years before and from thousands of miles away. However, they remained my private encounters.

Listening to other cellmates' stories was amusing, though, and many of them could qualify for a book of short stories about the magic and mystique of relationships – but my stories would never be mentioned in that book.

I heard many tales from inmates about their encounters with prostitutes in Yemen. I used to think that our cities did not suffer as much as other parts of the world in this regard, but after treating two inmates with gonorrhoea I wasn't so sure.

But in addition to this type of sordid story, I also heard romantic tales, accounts of secret lovers and stories of broken hearts from those who had seen their young sweethearts get married before their eyes. Pious and zealous inmates listened with obvious interest before resuming their endless prayers.

There were also stories about men falling prey to predatory women. These were my favourite tales. It has always been my observation that women are stronger than men. Men appear stronger only when they have the upper hand financially, which is most often the case. When men and women are on the same ground, men stand no chance.

There is a Yemeni proverb: 'Men are like dogs. Wave to them to come, they come. Tell them to get lost, they leave.' I was 14 when I first heard this saying during a visit home from my studies in Cairo. The proverb was confirmed over the next five decades of my life, as I travelled the world.

My cellmates, who thought they were skilful charmers, should carefully revisit their records to find out how many times they were rebuffed or turned down. On the occasions when they were successful, they should have become aware of the subtle lures of women before they started bragging about their skills.

Relationships between women and men start with a wink or smile of encouragement. I often feared rejection, so I rarely pursued anything. I just sat there like a good dog.

Chapter 25

I was alone for hours after Menbehi had been taken away before a young man was thrown into the cell. This was Nader, who was covered with bruises from being hung by his wrists and beaten during his interrogation.

He worked the luggage inspection X-ray at Sana'a airport and was accused of allowing an ancient Jewish Torah scroll to be smuggled out of the country by Yemeni Jews leaving for Israel. When they arrived there, they were feted by prime minister Netanyahu, who proudly held aloft the ancient Torah they had brought with them. Nader was also accused of accepting bribes and spying.

"The Houthis felt humiliated and wanted a scapegoat," he explained. "They chose me because I was from Al-Hudaidah. My fellow workers were from Sana'a or from tribal and *sayyid* origins. They could have been responsible, but I was singled out. Besides, the Jews were asked to go to National Security headquarters with their luggage a day before their departure and then return to the airport the next day, leaving their luggage overnight to be loaded onto the plane for them. I'm only a scapegoat."

I complained once to a friend about the habit of northern tribesmen and army commanders of making trouble for people outside their region and seizing their belongings.

"You should consider yourself lucky in Taiz," this friend, an adviser to Saleh, told me. "In Al-Hudaidah and the Tihamah wadis, they kill people who do not readily give up their farms."

Another politician told me that his party leader complained to Saleh about looting and confiscation of farms in those areas, to which the president had answered curtly: "This subject is not for discussion. Tihamah is ours."

Nader had a degree in physics from Sana'a University, but the only job he could find was in the customs authority. His two brothers and sister all had university degrees and his sister had been elected as a delegate to the National Dialogue Conference. His wife was from a respectable Sana'ani family, who had been neighbours of theirs. His father was raised in Al-Hudaidah, where he became a member of the Socialist Party when it was still banned and, as a consequence, had been jailed in his youth. He later moved to Sana'a and, after unification, never missed a party meeting. As Nader and his siblings grew up, their father would often say to them, "I might not be able to provide you with a comfortable life, but I'll leave you all with education and university degrees".

Nader was in his late 20s, strong and agile, gentle and polite. After recovering from his beating, one day, when I pointed to a huge cockroach in the cell, he jumped up to catch it, then gently released it through the hatch – possibly the only person in the whole of Yemen who would save a cockroach. I was amazed at the conscientiousness of this young man, jailed under false pretences.

He told me how northern tribesmen tried to agitate the people of Tihamah against citizens from Taiz.

"Those officials stir us up against Taizis by claiming they all own shops and businesses, and we naively fall into the trap," he said. "Our main problem is that we aren't united, so those who get hold of government posts from the police and army use our dignitaries against us to write fake documents to take our lands in exchange for small rewards."

I agreed. "To be in a trade or profession isn't wrong," I said. "But getting a government or army post because you come from a certain tribe is wrong. And squatting on other people's land is wrong, too."

We agreed that we should stay in touch after our release.

Nader was taken away for interrogation twice during the following week, each time returning with more bruises and tearful sobs. With each passing moment, I could see him sinking deeper into depression, but I could do nothing. He started to hear his father's voice through the wall, imagining that he was also being interrogated and beaten up. These appeared to be honest delusions because Nader believed that we shared a wall with the jail's head office.

When I could finally get his attention, I said: "Nader, I've lost a lot, too. But I am determined to stay in one piece."

"I would too if I was accused of what you did. You'll leave this jail as a hero, but in my case they smeared my reputation and accused me of something shameful. Please, if you are released before me, go and talk to my wife and family, and tell them I did nothing wrong," he pleaded.

He was truly in torment over his ruined reputation. He missed his family, and the awful jail conditions deepened his loneliness. He began to bang his head against the wall. Amid long bouts of weeping, his delusions became more frequent and longer and he deteriorated rapidly.

I reached a point where I couldn't sleep, let alone escape into my imagination. My other defence mechanisms of stoicism and exercise also failed me. Nader's deteriorating condition was gradually wearing me down.

Finally, I could take no more. I convinced the jail authorities that, if Nader was moved to a more crowded cell, it would help alleviate his symptoms because he would be more stimulated. He was duly moved to the cell opposite ours, where he seemed to sleep most of the time. The guards thought that he was getting better, but I wasn't so sure.

He was replaced by Sami, another man in his 20s, who entered the cell gently massaging his jaw, where he had been punched – not by an interrogator but by a zealous inmate who didn't like the way he prayed.

"They took us both to the administration office to punish us: he got the heavier beating as they saved the lighter blows for me," he said with a mischievous grin.

The jailers had decided to separate Sami from his Salafi cellmate, which only ignited a new problem.

"I offered to move from the cell but the Salafi shouted that he didn't want to stay in the old cell, complaining that we weren't religious enough. He demanded to be moved in with you, Doctor," he said.

"Good grief!" I exclaimed. I really did not want to repeat the experience of being alone with a religious zealot in a tiny cell again. "Praise God that they brought you instead," I murmured.

When prayer time came, I silently stood up and began to pray alone. After I finished, Sami did the same.

"At last, I'll have some peace in this jail," he said happily afterwards. "I loved that you didn't invite me to pray. I'm sick of people telling me what to do and what not to do."

Sami told me that his father, who was originally from Dhamar governorate, had opened a home utilities repair shop in Sana'a.

"I was born in the old city of Sana'a. I talk like them and dress like them. I consider myself a Sana'ani. My mother is a Shareefah from Raimah, and I joined the Houthis for the fun of it. I even swore the oath of loyalty to a *mushref*. But when they wanted to send me to one of their battlefronts, I escaped."

Sami knew Houthi *zamel* by heart and would often chant.

"Houthis are dumb but their *zamels* are beautiful – they make you melt in exultation. Whenever I talk to Abu Shemakh, I make sure to deliver an appropriate line, and he always laughs and extends his fist to mine in solidarity," he said.

"Why were you jailed, if you are so friendly with Houthis?" I asked.

"I did nothing against Houthi or Saleh. All I did was chase a girl who wanted to climb the social ladder and make a fortune by forming an NGO. The girl said that she felt bad for Jewish children, who were not allowed to get a public education, so she created an NGO that advocated extending the same rights to Jews as everyone else. I told her that I felt the same for Jewish kids who could only watch their neighbours go to school every morning."

"That's funny! In a place where Houthis shout 'damn the Jews' and wish them death on every public occasion, you wanted to help Jewish children. Did you expect to get away with it?" I asked incredulously.

"All I wanted was to be near the girl. I was so keen that I even offered to join her NGO," he said, smiling. I couldn't prevent the smile on my own face from broadening. "Anyway, they forced her to stop her activities and demanded she appear each day at the National Security headquarters from early morning until evening. And she did. This was her sentence for trying to provide education to Jewish children. As for me, they brought me to this lousy jail," Sami said with a laugh. "My interrogator told me that I am the first person whose penis landed him in trouble for reasons of National Security! But all the jailers here like me and say I will soon be released."

Many young Yemenis were envious of those who built connections with Western NGOs. It was presumed to be a lucrative business, so they aspired to join the club, earning salaries in dollars and other perks, such as trips abroad. The girl that Sami chased thought that, if she adopted the cause of a local Jewish community, she would eventually make it to the top league of Western-sponsored civic activists. Sami just wanted to catch the girl.

"I want to be educated like you, although it's unlikely that I will finish my education because I have to work, but I want to know everything," Sami said to me one day, after bombarding me with questions about myself.

After this declaration, Sami always asked me to teach him about one thing or another. Following each of my 'lessons' about the history of Yemen and the world, he would declare that, as soon as he was released, he would "read a lot of books to become like you". Whenever I exercised, Sami would watch but not join in, and he told me that he had been in more than one cell with many inmates, "but you are tougher than the members of Al-Qaeda".

"Toughness is in the mind, not the body," I said, before explaining my technique for remaining strong through exercise, stoicism and contemplation.

We stayed together for one week, and then Sami was released. In comparison to other cells I'd been in, thanks to the company, it was a pleasant week.

****

One of the last prisoners I came to know during my time in jail was Hu, a German-Vietnamese dual national. He had studied in Germany, was married and had two children. But when his German wife deserted him and the marriage fell apart, he was broken-hearted and couldn't bear to stay in Germany, so he returned to Vietnam and remarried. Soon after, he was offered a job in Yemen by a German telecommunications firm to launch a new service for Saba Phone, which was owned by Hamid Al-Ahmar, the Islah leader who was the staunchest foe of Saleh and the Houthis.

On Hu's second day in Sana'a, Houthi forces took him from his hotel room, accused him of espionage and dropped him in my cell. He asked me to memorise the email address of his Vietnamese wife, wanting me to contact her after my release to tell her to approach a Turkish lawyer in Germany who could ask the German government to lobby for his release as a German citizen.

"Don't worry, you will be released soon," I said, trying to reassure him. "Houthis love Germany as it has often offered them political asylum in the past. The German government is cosier with Houthis than the rest of Europe."

For obscure reasons, the German government perceived Yemenis as more pro-Houthi than was actually the case. Thus, it had a good relationship with the Houthis and vice versa.

Hu was reassured a little, but it was difficult to explain Yemeni politics to him so he could understand why both he and I were in jail. In the end, I found that I could use Hu's dual nationality to explain a few basic things to him about the turmoil. Put simply, I couched it like this. Vietnam sorted itself out by force and implemented a one-party system, whereas Germany followed a social contract with a multiparty system.

However, Yemen was neither one nor the other: Houthis wanted to rule by force as a superior, divine entity, while most Yemenis were struggling to get a social contract and equal citizenship.

"You could say that Yemen is experiencing the labour pains of giving birth to a social contract," I suggested.

Both of us thought that was a good enough explanation for the current troubles in Yemen.

****

On the 300th day of my captivity, I was taken without notice to the administration office, where the deputy officer said, while carefully studying my reaction, "You'll be released tomorrow".

I gave no reaction at all, just a nod indicating that I understood.

"Don't get excited. They may change their minds at headquarters," he warned.

I nodded again.

"Are you going to start writing again?" he asked with a faint smile.

"I don't need to. All the things that needed to be said, I have said already."

I was returned to the cell and just had time to bid farewell to Hu and collect my meagre possessions before I was blindfolded and handcuffed, put inside a dark metal box on the back of a prison car, and driven through the streets of Sana'a to the National Security headquarters.

Fortunately, the officials there did not change their minds and I was released – emaciated and with a long white beard – into the care of my two elder sons, who were waiting for me outside, ready to drive me off for a reunion with my wife.

My release was totally unexpected and came as a complete shock – albeit a very welcome one – to me and my family. I had no idea why I had been freed so suddenly; other inmates who had been let out had departed with similar lack of notice or (as far as I knew) explanation.

Once out, I soon learned that dozens of people at home and abroad had been campaigning for my freedom and had protested my incarceration with the Houthis. I still do not know if any one person was pivotal to my release, but I remain profoundly grateful to everyone involved for their ultimately successful efforts.

One of my first actions as a newly free man was to fulfil my promise to Hu and contact his wife. He was also released, just two weeks after me.

PART 2: NOTES ON THE UPRISING

War comes to Taiz

The war inside my city started with an assault by Houthi and Saleh-aligned forces in March 2015.

Like the rest of the country, Taiz had been embroiled in unrest for years, ever since protest marches against the Saleh regime first erupted in 2011. Between then and the 2014 coup, the Houthis had been busy expanding from their domain around Saada. They reinforced their relations with the sayyids in the northern tribal areas and sent emissaries to places like Taiz and Aden. They blended and bonded with the remnants of the old guard – the local sayyids who became Houthis. They had been present at our protests with their own tents and propaganda for years, leading up to the Houthi-Saleh coup.

Republican Guard forces loyal to Saleh were already stationed throughout the city and governorate, as they were throughout the country. In our city they were stationed in the Republican Palace, on Mount Sabr, in the broadcasting station, at the old airport and the new one, and in Al-Ganad, Al-Mafraq, Mokha and Thu Bab. Each unit was headed by a Saleh family member or a tribal ally. In addition, there were well-armed Central Security forces led by Saleh's nephew, Yahya.

The Houthi-Saleh coup against the transitional political process began on 21 September 2014. Saleh contributed 26 brigades of former Republican Guards, with Houthi militia acting as the spearhead.

From February 2015 the Houthis and Saleh despatched more forces to Taiz by air – which most people saw as a sign that the city would be used as a staging point from which to attack Aden and seize President Hadi, who had fled there earlier that month. The Houthis intended to impose their culture, identity and sect on our regional community. They had been trained and armed by the Al-Quds Brigade of Iran's

Revolutionary Guard and Hezbollah of Lebanon.

Facing this formidable and well-equipped Saleh-Houthi coalition were the brave, untrained young men of Taiz, armed with only a few Kalashnikovs and a dwindling supply of ammunition. These men defending Freedom Square were aiming to prevent the sort of violence that had erupted there in 2011 when protestors' tents were burnt and shots were fired during Friday prayers.

Streets around the huge Central Security camp in the centre of the city were occupied by protesters to block the entry of the coup forces expected to arrive from the airport. Protestors were dispersed by tear gas, thugs and soldiers in uniform – with several shots fired on the peaceful protesters from the surrounding buildings.

That day, every shade of Saleh antagonist, leftist and Islamist, decided they would participate in the uprising; Zandani even made it a religious duty. This would have been unthinkable in 'normal' times – a bearded man linked to Osama bin Laden who praised leftists, nationalists and liberals. After that, Islah and the Muslim Brothers placed all their resources in the service of the protests that eventually ended the 33-year-long Saleh era.

Women were prominent throughout the Freedom Square protests. Many came with their children and it was considered extremely daring that both men and women continued to protest while the Houthi-Saleh reinforcements poured into the city.

There was no armed struggle in Taiz apart from this – although Brigade 35, led by Major Colonel Adnan Al-Hammadi, camping in the old airport west of the city, did rebel for several weeks. This action certainly caught the imagination of the people of Taiz because he was one of the rare Taizi officers with such a rank.

The protests went on for three days until Shawki Ahmed Ha'el Sa'eed, the governor of Taiz, resigned. On the fourth day, 26 March, as Saleh-Houthi troops entered Aden, the Saudis started an air campaign against Yemen. The Saudi-led intervention, codenamed Operation Decisive Storm, saw Saudi Arabia leading a coalition of nine countries from the Gulf and Africa in response to calls from President Hadi for military support after he was ousted by the Houthis and fled to Saudi Arabia. The military intervention was to continue until the ceasefire announced during the Covid-19 pandemic in early 2020.

Seeds of the uprising

Saleh had been forced to resign as a result of the popular uprising that began in Taiz in 2011, just two weeks after Mubarak in Egypt resigned because of the uprising there. Once the young men of Taiz poured into the city's streets that midnight, they never returned to their homes. The countdown to the end of the Saleh era had begun.

The first protests in Taiz's Freedom Square echoed with the same shouts and slogans that first appeared in the streets of Tunis at the outbreak of the Arab Spring when the people overthrew President Zine Al-Abidine Ben Ali. Their slogan echoed across the streets of Cairo and eventually reached my hometown.

Two weeks later, a similar protest erupted in Change Square in Sana'a, although the leadership of the Islah Party was hesitant to demand the regime's fall, instead calling for its reform. Since the late 2000s, Islah had been the dominant opposition coalition and was also known as the Joint Meeting Parties (JMP). It formed after President Saleh was challenged in Yemen's 2006 elections by Faisal bin Shamlan, the former oil minister from Hadhramaut who had a reputation for integrity.

At the beginning of the 2011 protests, Islah was wary that its own Salafist wing, led by Abdul Majeed Al-Zindani, would object to public calls for the fall of the regime, thus risking a split. However, Al-Zindani decided to give the protesters his blessing, telling them "You are an invention that we never conceived". An hour before, Al-Zindani had stood beside President Saleh at a televised meeting with Sunni clerics (*ulama*) at which he urged them to issue a *fatwa* against the protests in order to avoid civil strife.

Back in 2006, the same *ulama* sided against candidate bin Shamlan, who was supported by the Muslim Brotherhood wing of Islah, while Al-Zindani's Salafist bloc remained loyal to Saleh. Their loyalty was rewarded with preferential treatment, especially for graduates from Iman University, Al-Zindani being its founder and dean.

Tensions only started during the latter half of Saleh's rule, when he allowed different elements to import dangerous ideas from outside. Al-Zindani and the Salafists brought Wahhabism from Saudi Arabia, while the Houthis brought Shia political ideology associated with Iran's Revolutionary Guard and Lebanon's Hezbollah.

This created a dangerous, combustible mix that Saleh could no longer manage. In fact, he put the whole country at risk by willingly exploiting religious divisions for his own personal advantage.

After 2006, Zaydi clerics deeply resented Saleh's willingness to hand control of the country's judiciary to Al-Zindani's Salafists, so they began to form closer relations with the Houthi rebel movement in Saada.

From 2004 to 2010, Saleh's regime and the Houthi rebels engaged in a series of armed conflicts against each other, but it was the popular protests of 2011 that forced him to resign. It was at this point that he formed an alliance with the Houthis in order to gain support to plot his return to power.

By then, Al-Zindani had joined the popular uprising against Saleh, after which he retreated to his home north of Sana'a, where battles raged for more than a year between local tribes and the Yemeni Republican Guard under the command of Saleh's son, Ahmad.

Al-Zindani had good reason to take refuge in his homeland. He had been declared a terrorist by the US thanks to his close connection to Osama bin Laden going back to the 1980s, when he helped him recruit Arab mujahideen for the anti-Soviet jihad in Afghanistan. While he was an ally of Saleh, Al-Zindani was protected from American sanctions, but now that equation had changed.

In late May 2011, a brief military uprising played out in Sana'a, as

Saleh's forces targeted the family of the late Abdullah bin Husayn Al-Ahmar, the paramount sheikh of the Hashed tribe, founder of Islah and a former speaker of the House of Representatives. A week later, a bomb exploded inside the presidential palace mosque during Friday prayers, killing the imam and gravely injuring Saleh.

Sectarian background

For centuries, Yemen's Zaydi *sayyid* clerics exercised monopoly control over the judiciary in the country's tribal areas. During imamite dynasties, the Zaydi *sayyids* also occupied judicial posts in Shafe'ei regions. Shafe'ei is a Sunni school of Islam followed by the majority in Yemen, while Zaydis are part of a moderate branch of Shia Islam that has different historical roots from the Shia of Iraq, Syria and Lebanon. Zaydism originates from followers of a rival fifth imam who lived in the eighth century, Zayd ibn Ali ibn Husayn.

As a result, Zaydis are sometimes called 'Fivers' to distinguish them from 'Twelvers' in Iraq, Syria and Lebanon who descend from followers of the 12th imam. Beginning in the 10th century, Zaydis began settling in and around the city of Saada in Yemen's northern mountains. After a few centuries, as their teachings were adopted by major local tribes, Zaydi imams began to extend their rule over wide regions of the country, including areas inhabited by the Sunni Muslim majority.

Throughout Yemeni history, there was never a sharp divide between Zaydi and Shafe'ei like the historical divisions between Shia and Sunni in Iraq, Syria and Lebanon. There was a certain antipathy and hidden disenchantments, but it is equally important to stress that it can never be described as comparable to the striking differences between the Jaaferi Twelvers and the staunch Sunnis or Salafists in Iraq, Saudi Arabia or Iran.

As long as Yemen remained relatively isolated from politics elsewhere in the Arab and Muslim world, it enjoyed relatively high levels of inter-sectarian peace and harmony. My own view is that, in Yemen in particular, the perceived schism between Sunni and Shia is not very important. In fact, I would go as far as to say that the majority of Muslims do not care about it.

The real issue is Iran. Sectarianism suits Iran's political purposes, exploiting it to incite minorities and then to train, arm and finance them to turn against their own people and act as instruments of Tehran. It was a surprise to us to find out that Iran's mullahs and Revolutionary Guards managed to lure the Zaydi sayyids to cosy up with them against the people who they were living with.

Saleh's return

If it were not for Saudi Arabia, Saleh would not have survived his injuries from that 2011 explosion.

When King Abdullah arranged for his medical evacuation to Riyadh, Saleh was septicaemic and had extensive burns over his body and a piece of shrapnel touching his heart. He underwent several operations including extensive skin grafts.

As a result, he was able to return to Sana'a after only a few months. Hundreds of thousands of bullets were fired into the air by jubilant tribesmen when he returned. Saleh claimed that he was back with "a fresh olive branch and the dove of peace", yet that very night he set about destroying the protest site in Change Square.

He was soon to unleash his militarised might, each division commanded by family members and cronies. We later learned that his use of force had the tacit support of the Saudi government and Western allies, as long as it continued for only one day.

This led to one of the bloodiest nights in Sana'a's recent history. Casualty numbers are not known for sure, but we do know that all the protestors' tents were set ablaze and the streets were turned into a wasteland by a bulldozer. Nonetheless, Saleh failed to remove protesters from Change Square due to the intervention by General Ali Mohsen's troops and armed supporters of Islah.

The protests in Change Square endured until Saleh agreed to step down, which he did in exchange for political immunity and the right to continue playing a role in Yemen's future. In November 2011, he signed the document that formalised his resignation at a ceremony in Riyadh in the presence of King Abdullah and foreign representatives.

Toppling the transitional government

Under the deal mediated by the GCC, Hadi became interim president in February 2012 after winning a referendum by a landslide. The coalition government under prime minister Mohammed Salim Basindawah included Islah and Saleh's General People's Congress (GPC) and was tasked with following the outcomes dictated by the National Dialogue Conference (NDC), which had been attended by delegates from all regions of the country.

Although president, Hadi had no influence over Basindawah. They had not even met since the oath-taking ceremony. Sheikh Hameed Al-Ahmar was the real influence behind the scenes, ordering Basindawah to appoint his secretary as head of the prime minister's office. Al-Ahmar effectively ran the government and in certain areas was more influential than the president, while the PM was a mere puppet. Neither Al-Ahmar nor Basindawah turned up to the ceremony for the conclusion of the National Dialogue outcomes, which was a very important day for the interim transitional period and the entire history of Yemen.

The NDC faced many obstacles, particularly when in January 2014 it agreed a new federal constitution, but it could not agree on the number of federal regions. Outside the NDC, a committee appointed by Hadi decided upon a six-region federal design comprising an autonomous region of Taiz and the midlands called Al-Janad; two regions in the south and east of the country called Aden and Hadhramaut; one region on the west coast called Tihama; one in the central desert called Saba; and one in the northern mountains from Dhamar through Sana'a to Saada, called Azal.

Both Saleh and Houthi leaders refused to accept the NDC's recommendations, especially the proposed six-region federal state. Saleh opposed federalism in principle, often speaking in conspiratorial terms about outside plots to divide and weaken Yemen. Houthi leaders did not accept their homeland of Saada being landlocked inside the proposed Azal region and wanted an expanded port on the Red Sea. President Hadi promised that the boundaries of the proposed regions would be adjusted to answer these objections.

The NDC proposals appeared reasonable to me, particularly its calls for respect for human rights, transparency in government finances, independence of the judiciary and building a real security apparatus and a real national army. The vast majority of my fellow citizens in Taiz felt the same way.

But Saleh and the Houthis refused to compromise and, in early 2014, armed Houthi rebels advanced toward Sana'a. In February, they destroyed the home of the late Sheikh Abdullah bin Husain Al-Ahmar in Amran governorate. In mid-summer, with support from army factions loyal to Saleh, they seized the governorate's capital of Amran and its army base before entering the city with direct help from Saleh's forces in September, seizing control of various ministry buildings.

The UN envoy overseeing the transition attempted to save the process by negotiating the formation of a new coalition that included Houthi representatives, but this failed when in December Saleh and Houthi forces attempted to block President Hadi from establishing the six-region federal constitution as law.

In January 2015, Houthis kidnapped Hadi's chief of staff, Ahmad Awad bin Mubarak, who was in charge of presenting the draft constitution to the House of Representatives. By the end of the month, Hadi and the new prime minister, Khaled Bahah, were placed under house arrest and forced to resign. The Saleh-Houthi coup was complete, and what had been a relatively peaceful political transition was over.

The coup opposed both the GCC plan and the NDC recommendations, but both Saleh and the Houthis primarily wanted political revenge. The Houthis sought retribution for the reverses they had suffered since the collapse of the Zaydi imamate in 1962, when a popular revolution led to republican rule.

Once Hadi managed to escape south to Aden, where he reclaimed his role as president, Saleh and Houthi leaders launched a full-scale war in an attempt to overrun the middle of the country around Taiz and southern regions around Aden.

Saleh's snake dance

In early 1994, when it was clear that Saleh intended to launch a war against leaders of the Yemeni Socialist Party in the South, I founded the January 18 Committee to Support the Document of Pledge and Agreement in my hometown of Taiz.

Meeting in the Medical Association Building, we attracted support from members of the Socialist, Nasserite and other small parties, as well as the non-partisans of the 'silent majority'. Together, we drafted an anti-war petition that was signed by 100,000 people. Similar petitions were then launched by peace activists in Sana'a and Aden.

We realised that Saleh was not satisfied with Yemeni unity based on consensus and democracy. He wanted his political partners from the former South Yemen to submit to his personal rule and pave the way for a family dynasty.

Our grass-roots peace movement attracted widespread media attention inside and outside the country during the early months of 1994. Saleh was furious and, in order to diminish our growing influence, created the Ramadan 10 Committee to Support the Document of Pledge and Accord, which preached a message opposite to ours. Its members included his ruling party, Mu'atamar (Congress) and Islah, which was linked to the Muslim Brotherhood.

Saleh's modus operandi had always been to use tribalism to his political benefit, pitting one tribe against another and bestowing favours to curry support. One example of this was his manipulation of Sheikh Al-Ghouli, a minor leader from the Ghoulah tribe from north Amran, whose loyalty he bought through various patronages. Sheikh Al-Ghouli had a history of switching allegiances, a typical opportunist who was prepared to change his colours depending on who was paying. He once belonged to the Socialist Party but, during the 2014 siege of Amran, was paid by Saleh to support the Houthi militias as they advanced on Sana'a. Indeed, his appearance at Amran was the earliest indicator that Saleh was allowing Houthis to benefit from political alliances that he had nurtured over four decades.

Houthi tribal militia besieged the capital from four directions. Heavily armed and backed by factions of the army still loyal to Saleh, they approached the capital parroting the peaceful slogans shouted by young Yemenis during the Arab Spring.

There were many such instances of him bending even senior northern sheikhs to suit his dynastic aims. For example, Saleh formed alliances with Hashed tribal Sheikhs Kahlan Abu Shawareb and Mashreqi by arranging marriages to two of his daughters. Both were used to undermine the authority of Al-Ahmar, the 'Sheikh of Sheikhs'. So too was Sheikh Gulaidan – also from the Hashed tribe – who was bribed to turn his back on Al-Ahmar with a government post in Aden and a construction contract.

So many things about Yemen's revolution were mocked and degraded in this way. Saleh had always claimed that Yemen was a republic at the same time as planning to make the presidency a dynasty for his sons to inherit. Houthi leaders would also talk about a 'republic' while seeking to create an Iranian-style Islamic state run by their own version of the ayatollahs – Zaydi imams from their own ranks.

A similar example of the degradation of democracy was Saleh's strategy of mimicking political parties, grass-roots movements and even NGOs. He would set up organisations with a similar name to sow confusion and create the false impression that he enjoyed broad support. You name it, he cloned it.

From as far back as 1990, Saleh extolled national unity, but he was always working to undermine it. In the same way, he was now calling for the peaceful transition of power but was actually using armed force to hang on to it. And, while describing the army as belonging to the nation, he was all the while appointing confederates from his family and tribe as commanders. Saleh never stopped plotting how to hold onto power.

The Houthi advance on Amran was possible once they overpowered the centre of Salafi strength in Dammaj, Saada governorate, the site of the Saudi-funded Salafist Institute, in late 2013. Once the Salafists had been forced out, Houthis destroyed the institute and other Salafi buildings and began a campaign of persecution against the remaining residents.

Objections were initially raised on social media and by Islah, but these voices virtually ceased when the US Chargé d'Affaires, Karen Sasahara, linked the Salafi Institute to terrorism in Europe and America. She also commented that the Houthis posed no threat to the US. The message was clear and critics fell silent, including Islah. America had spoken.

Al-Hajouri, the head of the Salafi Institute, eventually fled to safety in Saudi Arabia. The Houthis were euphoric after demolishing a site used by their ideological and sectarian enemies. They were even more pleased by the US government's approval, notwithstanding their 'Death to America' sloganeering.

Believing they deserved a reward for this 'service to the West', they subsequently targeted the sons of Sheikh Al-Ahmar, enemies they had in common with Saleh. Advancing to Beit Al-Khamri, a village to the north of the capital, they blew up the Al-Ahmar homestead, posting a video clip of the attack on social media with the perpetrators shouting 'Bye-bye, Hassonah!'', referring to Hussein Abdullah Al-Ahmar, who had been paid by the Saudis to recruit Yemeni tribesmen to the Salafi Institute. This was a final blow to the House of Al-Ahmar and possibly to the Hashed tribal confederation, which was unlikely to ever again designate a paramount sheikh to rebuild the confederation.

All that now stood between the Houthis and Sana'a was the city of Amran, which was defended by General Al-Qushaibi of the national army. He was a close ally of Yemen's military strongman, General Ali Mohsen Al-Ahmar. General Qushaibi's daughter was married to Al-Zindani's son, showing the overlapping circles of Yemeni politics.

Illustrating the complex and volatile pattern of alliances and betrayals, during the siege of Amran the Houthis were helped by the same branches of the Hashed tribal confederation that Saleh had dismembered from the House of Al-Ahmar.

At some point in the past, Saleh had been closely allied with all the players named here: Al-Ahmar, Al-Hajouri, Al-Qushaibi, Ali Mohsen and Al-Zindani. Decades earlier, Saleh had encouraged the Salafist Al-Hajouri (and before him Al-Wad'ei) and (Muslim Brother-Salafist) Al-Zindani to spread their brands of Sunnism to weaken the grip of Hashemi sayyids and tribal sheikhs. In the end, he made a U-turn by uniting with former enemies among the Hashemi political establishment against his former allies in the Hashed tribal establishment and the Salafi movement.

Saleh was a master of divide-and-rule, always finding ways to exploit the weaknesses of his stronger opponents. He once famously said that, as leader of the country, he "danced on the heads of snakes" – meaning Yemenis. It was a nickname that stuck.

Ali Mohsen: Yemen's 'strongman'

General Ali Mohsen Al-Ahmar had been a life-long confederate of Saleh and the leading member of the so-called Sanhan Tribal Kitchen that ran Yemen from behind the scenes. But he had ditched Saleh on 21

March 2011, three days after the Dignity Friday massacre in Sana'a's Change Square in which Saleh loyalists opened fire and killed 52 protestors, 27 of them from Taiz.

Change Square attracted everyone with a grudge against Saleh, including those who wanted to take his place. All General Mohsen's long-standing friends – the Al-Ahmars, Al-Zindani and tribal supporters of Islah – were there. Even Ali Mohsen's sworn enemies, the Houthis, were in attendance, though confined to their own enclave.

When General Mohsen and his soldiers joined the protestors after the Dignity Friday massacre on 18 March 2011, he became known as a defender of the protestors. The Saudis were unamused by Mohsen's new role but, because of the shifting sands of Yemeni politics, they would later save his life when the Saudi ambassador helped smuggle him out of the country in September 2014 after the Houthis took Sana'a.

Qat and chat

Ahmad Al-Mosawa was a sayyid judge who would later give up his position to devote himself to Houthi affairs. He would come to my occasional Thursday *magyal* to talk while chewing qat, one day bringing with him a fellow *sayyid* judge from the north of the country. His guest's family name was Al-Sharafi and he was clearly a Houthi supporter.

"As you see, we are most tolerant," Al-Sharafi said to me as we chewed qat. "We can become friends and allies with secular parties. We proved it in Syria, where Hezbollah and the secular Ba'ath leaders became our strongest allies."

I was quick to recognise the significance of tying Yemeni Houthis to the Lebanese Hezbollah, both backed by the governments of Syria and Iran.

Both men thought of me as a secular, progressive modernist and clearly wanted to impress me with their talk of tolerance, as well as their credentials, affiliations and alliances. They believed that they could attract me by speaking of secularism, but I found the whole charade tiresome. I couldn't be bothered to refute their arguments, which were unfortunately very persuasive with many others in Yemen.

At another qat gathering, Al-Mosawa brought a young man named Hakimi, who was the son of a colleague of mine whose family I knew well.

"Let Houthis have a go at ruling the country. Why not? They couldn't possibly be worse than Saleh and the tribes," he opined.

"Your grandfather Abdulaziz was a friend of my father and your father is a colleague of mine," I told him. "I know very well that all your family are proud Taizis and Nasserites. Does your father know that you're a Houthi? I'm sure of one thing. If your grandfather came out of his grave, he would be shocked listening to what you say, and he would rush back to his grave to hide from you."

Houthi leaders never shied away from jumping onto as many bandwagons as possible, attempting to control the reins through their rhetoric while steering simultaneously in every direction. They sucked the sap from every branch of the tree of Yemen, and then happily cut off the branches once they had served their purpose. In political terms, the Houthis' approach to rule was a carbon copy of Saleh's snake dance.

A presidential summons

Back in 1994, I was driving home from a lunch in Taiz when I saw a friend coming in the opposite direction. He motioned for me to stop, jumped out of his car and told me he had been looking for me everywhere.

"Turn round. I've just come from the president's *magyal* and he demanded that I come back with you."

"Do you think I should? I know he's pretty angry with me," I replied.

A few months earlier, the proprietor of *Yemen Times*, Abdulaziz Al-Saqqaf, had warned that the protest movement I had helped to establish had peeved Saleh, who I had known since the 1970s when he was the military commander in my hometown.

"I think the president is planning something bad for you. So be careful!" warned Al-Saqqaf.

At the time I thanked my friend. After thinking about it, I realised that my earlier actions had come back to bite me. I was compelled to go back with my friend and sit and chew qat with the president. I did not even have a chance to go home and change into a fresh *thobe*.

Whenever he stayed in Taiz, Saleh usually held his *magyal* in the Republican Palace, which was on the side of Mount Sabr, immediately to the east of the city. All important political meetings took place there. But that day, Saleh was conducting the business of the nation at his private home in Akamat Al-A'kaber (The Rat Hill), which had been built with public money by the Department of Military Logistics and Supplies.

Saleh sat in the reception room, facing panoramic windows overlooking the city. On the opposite side of the room in front of the windows were two of his loyalists. My friend and I were directed to sit between them. I was the odd one out, and not simply because I was wearing Western clothing. Saleh saw I had no qat and gave me some from his personal stash.

These were tense times in the middle of July 1994. Saleh was in the process of winning control of the southern half of the country and eliminating the Yemeni Socialist Party, which had been an effective opposition in the south and east. Its leader, Ali Salem Al-Beidh, who had unified the country with Saleh, had fled to Oman.

The president took a telephone call. It was easy to deduce what it was about.

"Tell the Omanis the fugitives should be returned," I heard him say. "They are wanted for justice. They don't qualify for political asylum. As for the arms they took, they should be returned immediately. They are the property of the Yemeni army and should be handed back without fail. The Omanis know what I am capable of."

The Omani government not only returned the arms, including jets, but also rebuilt Al-Haswa power station in Aden, which Saleh's air force had destroyed during the war. Implicit in his threat was unleashing his Afghan Arab fighters into Oman's Dhofar region.

As we sat, a second call came – from New York, concerning Haidar Al-Attas, the former socialist prime minister of South Yemen, and his efforts to convince the UN Security Council to help the southern secession. Saleh had previously sent his ally Abdulaziz Abdulghani, the former PM of North Yemen, to act as a foil to Al-Attas at the UN and managed to prevent the Security Council from taking any action.

Similarly, former prime minister Abdulkareem Al-Iryani was sent to Washington. Earlier in the war, the US had warned Saleh against sending his armed forces into Aden, but now, in exchange for giving Saleh a green light to take control of the city, they asked Al-Iryani for five guarantees: to pardon the 16 southern politicians in exile who had been sentenced to death; to maintain a multiparty democracy; to maintain a free market; to preserve free passage through the strait of Bab Al-Mandab; and to show goodwill towards Israel.

Saleh agreed without hesitation – and, once Aden had been taken, his jubilant supporters hailed him as the 'Knight of All Arabs'. However, for the majority of Yemenis, the reaction was one of horror at the violence and looting committed by his troops.

At the UN, Lakhdar Brahimi from Algeria, the UN Special Representative for Yemen, announced that the Yemen file was closed. He was later awarded the country's highest honour by Saleh, who was very grateful for his role in ending the stalemate.

Hearing the triumphant tone of Saleh's phone call, I realised that I was probably going to be spared a reprimand, so felt much more relaxed – though still a little edgy. After the call, Saleh rose to his feet and beckoned me to follow him into a side room, where we sat alone.

"You have been fooled by Mohammed Abdulmalek Al-Mutawakkel and Abdulrahman Al-Jifri!" he said, without pleasantries.

Trying to collect my thoughts, I changed the subject and, to keep him off-balance, went on the offensive.

"We made Al-Thawrah Hospital the best in all Yemen when we founded Taiz Health Charitable Society," I said. "But you dismantled our work and shuttered the society, disrupting our lives and those who depended upon us for good healthcare. Not only that, but I was a friend of and in the same class at secondary school as Dr Abdulkader Homarah. He was my colleague in Taiz hospital, and you helped his murderer escape justice."

The president's face changed as he went on the defensive.

"Al-Thawrah Hospital? That wasn't me! It was the folks from the Yemeni Socialist Party, your own colleagues," he claimed.

I smiled and muttered: "What socialists? And what party?"

He returned my expression. I knew that he remembered everything he did. The tale of Al-Thawrah Hospital in Taiz was an example of Saleh's standard tactics of making Yemenis fight each other for his gain.

He looked at me more seriously.

"The culprit's only brother died as we stormed Al-Anad air base, so do you still want me to execute the murderer and leave his father without any sons?" he asked.

I left soon after, thinking sadly about my friend. His killer was an army lieutenant who had chased his victim along Jamal Street in Taiz one afternoon in 1984. He stopped Dr Humairah and stabbed him with a dagger, piercing his femoral artery, as he had learned to do in Special Forces training. With pistol in hand, he prevented anyone from coming near my friend, who bled to death.

Although the lieutenant was found guilty and sentenced to death (a verdict that was upheld on appeal – surprisingly, given the political atmosphere), President Saleh pardoned him.

Rashad, the friend with whom I clicked

Rashad Al-Alimi, the Deputy Prime Minister for Security and Defence and Minister of Local Administration, was one of those injured with Saleh in the 2011 palace attack that sent the president to Saudi Arabia for emergency treatment of his near-fatal injuries.

I first met him in 1996 and we clicked immediately. This was shortly after his appointment as chief of public security in Taiz. We could talk for hours about all manner of things and I was always flattered by his interest in my opinions. I became even closer to him and his family when I became his mother's physician.

In 2001 he was asked to head the Ministry of the Interior. Rashad was a workaholic, on whom President Saleh soon grew to rely more and more. Indeed, he was one of the few officials that Saleh didn't mock. While he was away in the capital, I would keep an eye on his mother's welfare and each time he returned to Taiz we would spend long hours chatting over a barbecue in my garden.

Rashad told me a fascinating story that explained much about Yemen. Apparently, Sheikh Abdullah Hussein Al-Ahmar's sons would habitually drive recklessly about the capital, ignoring any police checkpoints. On one occasion, the police tried to stop an Al-Ahmar car, whereupon there was a shooting, with casualties on both sides. The wounded Al-Ahmar protagonists were put in hospital under guard, but the following day they were seized by their compatriots and secreted away in Sheikh Al-Ahmar's compound.

"What kind of Ministry of Interior do we have?" President Saleh angrily demanded of my friend.

"Mr President, would you give me a free hand and your support if I act?" asked Rashad.

The president agreed, so Rashad planned an operation to counter the powerful Al-Ahmar family, arresting five of the sheikh's main henchmen at their homes at dawn, seriously undermining his ability to handle his personal interests. Sheikh Al-Ahmar sent an envoy to Rashad to ask for the release of his men, but he returned empty-handed. Then a more senior messenger was sent – also to no avail. Instead, the mighty sheikh had to approach the president and beg for a favour.

There once was a saying in Sana'a that 'Al-Ahmar is the Sheikh of Saleh, while Saleh is the President of Al-Ahmar', meaning that the two perceived each other as inferiors yet held each other in check. The plan Rashad devised to bring about a favourable resolution of the problem was previously unthinkable, because it was assumed that nothing could be done to alter the stalemate. To say the least, the president was pleased with the ruse and, of course, with Rashad, too.

The story demonstrates Rashad's best political traits. He came up with an effective manoeuvre to restrain Sheikh Al-Ahmar without resorting to violence. Rashad also charmed the two envoys, so the sheikh was not personally affronted.

Much later, in 2006, when Rashad was running Saleh's election campaign in Taiz, I asked him why he was doing so. Telling me he would happily change tack if I could suggest a better approach, he explained that he was doing so in order that he might be able to influence Saleh. He was also committed to serving Yemen to the best of his ability – and, not least, to benefit Taiz and the rural area of Al-Aloum, where he came from.

He did indeed have a road and electricity brought to Al-Aloum and was renowned for helping countless people from all across the country. He also tried his best to introduce gun controls, Yemen being just behind the US in terms of personal gun ownership with an estimated 60 million firearms in the country – roughly two for each man, woman and child. In some regions of Yemen, there are *souqs* where hand grenades and even RPGs are sold openly. Unfortunately, though, the legislation was defeated thanks to Sheikh Al-Ahmar's opposition.

Times changed drastically for my friend. Saleh's sons and nephews were not pleased with Rashad's growing popularity so, in 2008, they asked their father to remove Rashad from the Ministry of the Interior. Instead, he was appointed Minister of Local Administration – rather an empty job, although he was later promoted to Deputy Prime Minister for Security and Defence Affairs.

Hamoud of Freedom Square

Freedom Square was an idea borrowed from the Arab Spring demonstrations in Cairo. Our protests began on Tahrir Street in downtown Taiz, but in a few days moved to a larger, more suitable site located next to Safer Station. It inspired the whole country and led to similar sit-ins in other cities, including Sana'a.

On 29 May 2011, Brigadier Qairan, the city's security chief, ordered his men to attack Freedom Square. They set fire to tents, dismantled a field hospital, bulldozed the whole area and looted the nearby hospital. He stationed tanks and forbade gatherings of more than two people. These were dark days for the city of Taiz. Throughout the uprising, Fridays were always used as a day to show defiance, and sometimes hundreds of thousands of demonstrators showed up.

At home, my phones began to ring. Protestors were using the women's protest as a diversion to turn up in far larger numbers at Sa'elat Osaiferah, one of the concrete flood channels that criss-cross the city. This was just a few hundred metres from the destroyed Freedom Square.

I began to tweet about developments to the wider world. I hardly had time to eat or rest as I relayed the news in English while army reinforcements poured in and the protestors defended themselves.

"Large numbers of men, women and children flood Freedom Square and start a party under the protection of the People's Defenders," I tweeted.

This was a phrase I invented when I proclaimed my friend Hamoud Al-Mikhlafi the People's Defender.

I had developed a rapport with Hamoud over the course of many qat sessions and meetings. I would invite him to my house whenever I hosted foreign journalists or other guests who came to learn what people of different political inclinations thought about the revolutionary events in 2011. I did not belong to any political party and, as an independent, could be friendly with people of all political colours. He had been there, for instance, when I hosted Laura Kasinof, a journalist writing about the uprising for the *New York Times*.

Even though I initially named him as a key leader of the protest movement, I came to believe that no party or individual should take the credit. By this point the whole city could not tolerate Saleh and his northern tribal supporters controlling the country. Hamoud's men kept defending the crowds of demonstrators until Saleh resigned as president.

Later, Hamoud's brother, Dr Sadeq, was killed in violation of a tribal agreement. I contacted a friend who was a prominent member of Islah and asked him to help Hamoud. He refused, saying Hamoud had become too big-headed. It is likely that Saleh encouraged outsiders to kill the brother in retaliation for 'Sheikh' Hamoud's activism. Personally, I did not call Hamoud 'sheikh', but preferred to call him Brother, or Hamoud. 'Sheikh' is a tribal honorific, and we in Taiz are not a tribal people.

The same day that Freedom Square in Taiz was liberated – 3 June 2011 – Saleh and his companions were targeted by the explosion at the Presidential Palace in Sana'a. We never learned conclusively who was responsible, or whether the blast came from a bomb or a missile.

What happened in Taiz that Friday was perhaps the first time that its people ever resorted to using armed force to defend the state.

Taiz is unique in Yemen. Its people are generally the most civic-minded, well-educated and entrepreneurial. To us, armed rebellion is anathema. Because of this, Saleh thought he could beat us into submission with just a handful of tribal henchmen armed with nothing more than wooden batons. Little wonder, then, how jubilant we were when we took Freedom Square back.

Despite our local dislike of gun ownership and our objection to armed force, we were ecstatic when Hamoud Al-Mikhlafi turned up at the right time as leader of the People's Defenders. He organised a large group armed with rifles, knowledge of the city's terrain and support from community leaders who owned the buildings around Sa'elat

Osaiferah. From the rooftops of these buildings, they were able to win the battle against the security forces.

A year later, Laura Kasinof returned to Taiz as my guest. She was surprised to learn that Hamoud, the quiet man she had first met in my house, had become the armed liberator of Freedom Square.

Following the events of Freedom Square, Hamoud's fame grew and he gained legitimacy to act as a sort of arbitrator. Everyone who came to his house to settle disputes, including people from outside his region, referred to him as Sheikh Hamoud. The process generally worked well, and disputants left satisfied.

Over the next few days, the three of us met several times, discussing the events and celebrating the anniversary of the liberation, which eventually led to a lengthy article by Laura in the *New York Times* on 21 July 2012 in which she likened Hamoud to Robin Hood. One of my dinners was even mentioned.

Opposites meet: the governor and the liberator

I also invited Shawki Ahmed Ha'el Sa'eed, the governor of Taiz, to one of my dinners for Laura. From one of the wealthiest families in Yemen (the owners of HSA Group, the country's only multinational), Governor Shawki was a prominent banker, businessman and industrialist as well as leading the regional administration. He also had the reputation of being an effective arbitrator (but not among commoners) thanks to the political, commercial and familial influence he wielded.

Both he and Hamoud had risen to prominence in the same city at the same period of time, but otherwise they were polar opposites. Shawki was an aloof businessman who represented the establishment, while Hamoud was a true populist who could have become a warlord. Normally they would never have sat down to eat together and would more likely be squabbling over social media. I was particularly pleased, therefore, to have them both as my guests and to bring them together again at a subsequent meeting at the governor's palace.

I could clearly appreciate the gulf between the two men, but strongly believed that my country needed them both. I also had a specific proposal to put to Shawki that I thought would benefit him and Hamoud, as well as Taiz – and indeed, the whole country.

I couched my idea in suitably 'business' language, describing how there were lots of disputes about land and real-estate ownership. This affected the construction business and made Yemeni workers abroad shy away from investing in Taiz and in Yemen in general. Hamoud was accepted by the commoners and was a good arbitrator, effective at getting people to compromise. This worked much better than the labyrinthine courts of justice, avoided violence and offered a quick way to resolve land disputes. In the long run it would improve security, increase investment in the construction industry, decrease unemployment and encourage stability.

Both the governor and the People's Defender liked my idea and Shawki soon began sending cases to Hamoud for arbitration. But whatever good one does, things may end badly.

Unfortunately, the atmosphere in Taiz deteriorated as local branches of Islah, the Nasserites and Socialists ignored agreements with the governor because their party leaders in Sana'a forced them to adopt goals that were really of little local importance. Our concerns over stability did not impress many people in the capital.

After Saleh's resignation, Yemen had entered a so-called consensual political process based on power-sharing between the JMP and Saleh's ruling GPC party. Squabbles soon erupted over who got what political appointment at both national and provincial levels.

To my mind, Shawki and his family business were local assets as much as Hamoud was. I did not see the former as a GPC stooge, nor the latter as an Islah puppet – rather, both men were excellent exemplars of Taiz. The problem was that they disliked and distrusted one other.

Hamoud used to complain to me that the HSA Group funded Saleh – which, of course, they did; all businesses had to do likewise.

Nevertheless, they were 'one of us' and good for Taiz. Fortunately, the easy-going Hamoud was always receptive to my views. But Shawki thought Hamoud was a troublemaker who threatened stability – which was anathema to the business community.

When these differences came to the fore, I would listen to both of them and try to find mutually acceptable solutions. At the time I had not realised I possessed such political skill, so was both surprised and delighted when my suggestions worked. However, the situation in Taiz was deteriorating rapidly and rifts in their relationship began to appear. They would manage to get along for weeks at a time before distrust would reappear and I would have to start all over again.

Shawki thought that Hamoud could do more to control agitators – and was often right in his accusations, as Hamoud privately admitted to me. But Hamoud wanted an official mandate to do this and Shawki could not afford to grant one, since to legitimise one armed group over the others would have undermined his political authority.

As economic conditions deteriorated further, more and more people criticised the governor, but I felt strongly that if we could help Shawki succeed then Taiz might be spared the conflicts between the GPC and the JMP that were splitting every community and governorate across Yemen.

At some point, Shawki told me that 'they' were still intending to squash Taiz into the ground. I understood exactly who 'they' were – Saleh and his loyalists, who were determined to make Taiz pay because of its role in the 2011 uprising. Saleh was the first northern tribesman in history to rule Yemen and most of the northern tribes also believed that the people of Taiz had brought the Saleh era to an end. Houthis have similar thoughts, and infiltrated Taiz through local Sunni 'Friday *sayyids*' and others who were coached in Lebanon and Tehran. One of them, Same'i, was even given the power of a Yemeni satellite TV station based in Beirut. After the coup he was appointed to the Houthi Political Bureau. Although Same'i was nominally buddies with Hamoud and they even have a relationship through marriage, he was closer to

Shawki. This shows how politics are practised in Yemen – a point often misunderstood by foreign analysts who lecture us.

Governor Shawki tried his best to protect our city by negotiating the 'Charter of Honour', which was meant to persuade everyone in Taiz to work together to prevent political meddling from Sana'a. He sent me an early draft of the charter for my comments and I added a few amendments that I thought would please the protesters in Freedom Square.

Despite the charter being accepted by all sides, the governor was growing increasingly frustrated about Islah's persistent demands for government appointments. They went as far as staging demonstrations outside the HSA Group's headquarters, where they even openly insulted the governor's mother.

I phoned Mohammad Qahtan, the third-most senior Islah party official in the capital, and originally from Taiz, to demand he do something about this. He, too, was incensed with their behaviour and agreed that their obsession with securing public appointments was ridiculous – but the next day he called back and said he had tried his best but to no avail. The local Islah activists were adamant. For my part I was worried that, if they continued to pursue political power, they were jeopardising the charter, our local unity and the fortunes of Taiz.

Ideology is not for Yemen

What good has any political trend done for Yemen over the past 60 years?

Precisely none, and for much the same reasons. Whether it was Nasserites, Ba'athists, Arab nationalists, communists, socialists, political Shias, Salafists, Al-Qaeda, Islah or Houthis, all have failed to address adequately the country's economic underdevelopment and lack of progress.

Each of them is a foreign import, albeit with some tinkering to make them more appealing to Yemenis. But fundamentally they were principally serving foreign agendas and had little to do with our culture, heritage or well-being. Importing these ideologies has done little more than sow confusion and exploit divisions inside the country. The end result has been Yemenis fighting one another and a grave loss of life and destruction of property. What makes it even more absurd is that these ideologies are all pretty much dead and buried in their own countries of origin.

Before the 1960s, there was one fundamental problem in North Yemen: the sayyids and their tribal allies who were parasites upon the ordinary people, *ra'eiyah*, who farmed the fertile parts of the country.

Throughout history, the ordinary people had been the productive backbone of Yemeni society while the Zaydi *sayyids* lived in isolation in remote hilltop fortresses and caves. But whenever ruling dynasties collapsed, the Zaydi and their allies ventured into the agricultural regions, making it difficult for the peasantry to maintain the land, and often forcing them to head abroad, from which derives the reputation of Yemenis as a migrant people.

After the Ottomans left the country in 1918, Yemen suffered a political vacuum, which was quickly filled by the sayyids and the northern tribes, groups who had always prevailed through violence when the state failed and the rule of law was in abeyance.

In the 14th century CE, the great Arab scholar Ibn Khaldoun remarked that Arabs managed their conflicts through *asabiyyah*, which, simply put, means a strong bond through blood or regional relations.

The northern *sayyids* are glued through the bond that links them as the descendants of the Prophet, possessing a unique solidarity based on being more noble and racially superior to others due to this genealogical connection. While northern tribesmen are bonded by *da'ei* and *maghram* and by descent from a common grandfather, Zaydi *sayyids* are bonded by their link to the Prophet. They also believe in *khorouj*, which means rebellion against any ruler – even if he is himself a Zaydi *sayyid* imam – if he does not meet their requirements. That is why they have killed each other throughout their history.

Northern tribes believe strongly in *feid*, or war bounty. In times of famine or drought, they attacked the Isma'ilis or Sunnis under a *sayyid* jihad banner. In times of chaos, they just attacked without the need for any banner. In general, they thought it was better to legalise their hostility by labelling it as jihad, but often they didn't bother.

On the other hand, a *sayyid* could not become an imam or king without having the support of northern tribes. There is a symbiosis between northern *sayyids* and tribes. Ironically, the second most common cause of the killing of *sayyids* is the northern tribes. One cannot possibly understand the Houthi movement and their prominence if these two bonds are not appreciated. If or when this current unity between the two collapses, Houthism will end.

Da'ei and *maghram* exist only north of the Sumarah heights, which is consequently the *de facto* border between Sunni and Zaydi religious sects. Any region of Yemen which does not follow *dae'i* or *maghram* cannot be considered truly tribal because the essence of tribalism is *asabiyyah*.

The root of all Yemen's problems derives from the unequal distribution of resources and the power of conflicting groups. The dominance of the *sayyids* and northern tribes can never resolve Yemen's political problems because they thrive on exploiting these very inequalities. It is what they have always done.

What Yemen needs is, first and foremost, an egalitarian social contract based on the rule of law. After six decades of confusion and internal conflict, the Yemeni people managed to produce three core texts, each of which is true to our culture, heritage and well-being. These are the 1994 Document of Pledge and Accord, the 2004 Foundation Document of the Joint Meeting Parties (JMP) and the 2014 National Dialogue Outcomes. Each is 100 percent Yemeni, created through the participation of all parts of the political spectrum, including northern *sayyids* and northern tribesmen. They deal with the same national concerns, embrace the same national spirit, and form the foundation for a much brighter future.

It is good to know other people's ideologies and even to make use of certain elements. But it is harmful to import other people's ideologies and become more royal than the king and implement alien thoughts and ways in a deformed fashion into our social structure.

Remarkable women

Yemeni women were instrumental in the uprising, making quite remarkable contributions for such a gender-segregated nation.

Young men were certainly brave and daring, and many sacrificed their lives. But the bravery and sacrifices of women, although fewer in number, had a greater impact. Often, women could get away with things that men could not and would use this to their advantage. A case in point was the women's protest camp in Taiz established once Freedom Square had been cleared.

By a certain point, Saleh could take no more of this and reacted with levels of violence against women that would not previously have been countenanced. Much of this happened in Taiz, which had a reputation as a centre of independent thought, a characteristic that applies to our womenfolk as well as the men. The first woman shot dead by regime forces was in Taiz, which also has the dubious distinction of being home to the highest number of female deaths during the conflict.

This violence against women shocked the whole of Yemen. But instead of scaring protesters, it had the opposite effect. The reaction Saleh got was one of scorn and defiance.

In a gender-segregated country like ours, seeing women on the front line in marches and camping in the protest squares was shocking to some but exhilarating to others. These women belonged to all parties, though the majority of veiled protesters belonged to Islah. There were also hundreds of non-partisan women who contributed by donating money, cooking meals and baking cookies to sustain the protesters in Freedom Square.

All of these women made remarkable sacrifices, but two in particular stand out, both of them from Taiz: Amal Basha, who was named 'Arab Woman of the Year' by the non-profit organisation Takreem in 2013; and Tawakkol Karman, who won the Nobel Prize for Peace in 2011.

I met Amal during Ramadan in 2011 at a gathering of liberals and socialists in Taiz where we all chewed qat. In her home in Sana'a she would regularly host unsegregated qat sessions, which was very liberal in the context of our country. Not only did she go about her business unveiled, but she also did not wear a headscarf, which was practically heresy in Yemen.

Amal was born and brought up in Taiz and graduated from the American University of Beirut. After she moved away, she would return to Taiz often to visit her mother and promote gender equality issues, to which end she formed an NGO, Sisters Arab Forum for Human Rights. She said that she remembered seeing me when she was a teenager, and I recalled treating her mother.

Once when I invited her to my house, Amal first went upstairs to say hello to my wife and daughters before quickly coming back down to where the discussions and qat chewing were taking place. My daughters were really taken with her, never having met a Yemeni woman quite like her. However, when I described her visit to my sisters, they were less impressed, to say the least!

When I attended a Ramadan gathering that she hosted in a hotel on one of her rare visits to Taiz, one of the main topics of conversation was my other exemplar of remarkable Yemeni women, Tawakkol Karman. On this occasion, Tawakkol was the subject of a great deal of criticism from the other guests, who were mainly socialists – much of it, in my view, unfair and unsubstantiated. Stories circulated by the liberals and socialists at the gathering were that she was profiting from the uprising, keeping Qatari donations for herself and selling medicine intended to treat injured protestors.

I had my doubts about the stories. After all, Tawakkol had been living in a tent and had not been able to cook a meal at home for her children for months.

I thought that the stories were more about the distinct differences between the two women. Amal was an experienced social activist, was liberal in outlook and went about with her head uncovered. By contrast, Tawakkol was a relative newcomer who wore a *niqab*, and was at the opposite end of the political spectrum (though she did jettison the *niqab* after she had won her laureate, making do with a *hijab*). Their rivalry appeared fierce but, although Amal could be feisty, Tawakkol didn't retaliate, often saying, "I'm not in the business of answering back to those who attack me for no reason".

Unfortunately, Amal, who had been lauded in the West for her support of human rights and freedom of speech, ended up supporting a Houthi militia that trampled on the rights of Yemeni citizens. She was a *sayyid*, born and brought up in Taiz, who in the final analysis could not free herself from her northern origins and prejudices. It was sad to see such an intelligent and decent person fall into this trap.

Tawakkol Karman began challenging the Saleh regime because it lacked the basic requirements of good government. She and her supporters regularly protested at the Ministerial Council, which was often featured on Al Jazeera news. As a result, Saleh had her arrested. However, this just drew the world's attention to her cause, forcing him to release her the next day.

I later learned that the president had been under intense pressure from his closest advisers to release Tawakkol. But it was too late. She had already won the political contest because she gained enough fame from spending a single night in jail to become eventually one of the most prominent faces of the Arab Spring. When the protests reached Sana'a in mid-February, Tawakkol made herself a tent in the street and never left.

Anatomy of failure

It took less than three years for Yemen's political transition to fail – from Saleh's resignation on 23 November 2011 until the Saleh-Houthi coup began on 21 September 2014.

Many people outside Yemen applauded Saleh's decision to step down, believing it represented a peaceful way forward. But he still had control of the Republican Guard, the security forces, the Intelligence Agency and tribal allies. The resignation agreement granted him immunity from prosecution and allowed him a political role as head of the GPC party.

His signature was meant to end the so-called Yemen Spring that had started in February 2011, but he had other ideas. I say 'so-called' because protests in Yemen had started long before those in Tunisia, Egypt, Libya and Syria. Yes, we copied their sit-ins, banners and slogans and events were triggered by the resignation of Egypt's president, Hosni Mubarak. But we had been marching in the streets for years, ever since Saleh began playing with the constitution. By 2011, we were primed to force his hand and start a consensual process of political transition.

This process was UN-sponsored and backed by the US, the GCC states and others, with US Ambassador Gerald Feierstein a key figure in the process. Unfortunately, the transition was negatively impacted in 2013 when the Obama administration abruptly withdrew Feierstein after changing its regional strategy. Thereafter, the shift in US policy created a vacuum in Yemen that was immediately filled by the Houthi-Saleh alliance.

In February 2012, Hadi was elected president. We had to turn a blind eye to the fact that he had been Saleh's vice-president because what was most important was the end to Saleh's 33-year rule. Mohammed Salim Basindawa was nominated prime minister. However, the influence of Hamid Al-Ahmar meant he was ineffective. Like Al-Ahmar, he didn't care about the NDC or support its outcomes.

Hamid Al-Ahmar, a millionaire businessman and a son of the late

'Sheikh of Sheikhs' of the Hashed tribe, thought of himself as the real architect of the Yemeni uprising. His ambitions were to be the next peacock of the country. Early in the transition, Al-Ahmar visited Cairo, where he was given a warm welcome by President Morsi and the Muslim Brotherhood. On his return, Al-Ahmar's ambitions caused a schism in the JMP opposition coalition by alienating the socialist and Nasserite coalition partners, which came to haunt him later when they failed to support him when he and his family were under attack from the Houthis.

The position of defence minister went to Saleh's southern ally, Mohammad Nasser, who was a UAE puppet more than he was Yemeni general. He paved the way for the entry of Houthis into Dammaj, Beit Al-Khamri, Amran and Sana'a by colluding with Saleh and outside interests. This included the crown prince of Abu Dhabi, Mohammad bin Zayed, known for his antipathy toward Hamid Al-Ahmar and Islah, and Saudi Arabia's Khaled Al-Tuwaijri, who at the time was Chief of the Royal Court and the highest-ranking non-royal in the Kingdom.

Without any personal power base inside Yemen, President Hadi did his best to avoid antagonising the Saudis. He went along with everything they wanted until he found himself living under house arrest in the capital, when he refused to give the Houthis everything they wanted.

We do not know how President Hadi fled from Sana'a to Aden, but possibly someone paid a lot of money. What could Saleh and Houthi have been thinking at the time? 'Why not take the oil money and then hit President Hadi with an airstrike in Aden and follow up with a military takeover'? This is exactly what they tried.

But the Saudis had different plans. President Hadi fled to Riyadh, and on 26 March 2015 the Saudi-led Operation Decisive Storm was launched.

In the end, it was not Hamid Al-Ahmar who became the new peacock of Yemen, but Abdulmalek Al-Houthi. But he was a peacock presiding over a wasteland.

PART 3: A LETTER FROM CANADA

The panda leaves one cage for another

It was wonderful to be with my two sons in my own car leaving the National Security HQ in Sana'a and heading to see my wife after 300 days in dim, airless prison cells.

The streets were full of graffiti glorifying the two Husseins: one the grandson of the Prophet who is esteemed by the Shia' Twelvers of Iran, the other the eldest brother of Abdulmalek Al-Houthi, who they aspire to raise to the status worthy of another great-grandson of the Prophet.

"I'd rather have stayed in the prison than live with this absurd graffiti," I said.

"The mood and atmosphere in Sana'a have changed completely," my sons explained.

When we reached our apartment, my wife came to the main door smiling and in tears, pulled me into a loving embrace and hurried me inside to enjoy the feast she had prepared. There was a starter of *shafoot*, platters of meat, soup, vegetables, salads, hot *saltah* in a stone dish, fresh bread and *bint al-sahn* covered with the best Yemeni honey – a typical middle-class feast prepared for special guests. Indeed, a feast like this needed to be followed by a siesta and then some qat. I was reminded that many people around the world – and even some Yemenis – do not appreciate that the best thing about qat is the togetherness and the intimate conversations it engenders.

Such daily festivities continued for two weeks, until I realised that there was no way I could stay in Yemen. After my release, I met scores of family members, friends, politicians, human rights activists and officials, UN staff and many others I had not known before my ordeal. I was also in contact with many other influential people I would never have imagined speaking with over the phone and on social media – a true sign of the times.

At first this was flattering to my vanity. But I soon realised it was over the top when one dear friend said that I was 'an icon'. I felt this was meaningless and found myself likening this praise to being a cute panda in a cage, being smiled at before the spectators moved on to another exhibit or left the zoo to return to their everyday preoccupations.

Ideally, I would have liked to go back to my house in Taiz, a place I designed and built in preparation for the whims and interests of my old age, but there was no way to return there. The area was still occupied by Houthis and subject to continued fighting. Besides, there was no way for me to support myself there as I had lost my income and we had been living on our dwindling savings and forced to sell various assets.

However, the legitimate government and the Houthis were still engaged in negotiations in Kuwait, so it was peaceful enough for me and my wife to head abroad from Sana'a airport.

The credit for ending up in Canada goes to my daughter Nagwan. She had prepared for such a day by making us sign papers and providing documents from Yemen, and then preparing paperwork in anticipation of the day when we would finally agree to her plans. However, we did have to wait in Cairo for three months before we were granted a Canadian visa.

I arrived in Canada in September 2016 and immediately took great pleasure in the wide, blue skies of Calgary, my new home – especially after being locked for 10 months in dank prison cells. It is an exceptionally clean city and Canadians are without doubt the politest people in the world. My sons Mohammed and Ahmad joined us in Calgary in June 2019. As I write, Mustafa was in his third year studying microbiology at the University of Victoria in British Columbia.

Now I have a grandson from my son, two grandsons from my daughter in Canada, and a grandson and granddaughter from my daughter in the United States, who are all a great source of pleasure to me. Children are life-softeners and I have always believed they could give us far more than we ever gave them as parents. Of course, that is only if things go smoothly – otherwise they can become our greatest source of sadness and agony.

****

Amazingly, despite the fact that at the time of writing I am now in my fourth year in Canada, my youngest sister – who is still in Taiz – asks me on WhatsApp about the causes of shelling or gunfire she can hear from inside our family house in the old walled city. Thanks to social media, it takes me moments to find out and get back to her.

As I write this, my city Taiz is still – for the sixth consecutive year – under siege by the Houthis, with indiscriminate shelling and snipers using ordinary people for target practice. Apparently, they cannot resist the thrill of watching their victims fall when they pull the trigger.

On 24 June 2017 I had the opportunity to speak at the UN in New York, when I described Taiz as suffering a fate similar to Sarajevo. The difference is that Taiz does not have CNN broadcasting the awful events to the world in prime-time bulletins.

My appearance at the UN was one of the moments when I most felt like that cute panda in a zoo. My listeners thought I was clever and sincere, and I did manage to make them feel sad, albeit briefly, but then everyone smiled goodbye and that was that.

I follow every single incident in the whole of Yemen. It tortures me to follow the agonies that my people are going through. When I talk with compatriots, we often come to the conclusion that our problems stem from the lack of a social contract, poor governance and economic failure in our country. By overcoming these three basic challenges, we could have security, justice, education and other fundamental necessities.

After my daily trawl of news from Yemen, I move my attention to regional and international matters and how they play out in Yemen. The Arab regional powers are simply no match for Iranian shrewdness, focus and dedication. As Yemen sinks into its sixth year of civil war, Iran is dragging the Saudis into a quagmire using the Houthi movement, which

Iran has successfully turned into a replica of Lebanon's Hezbollah. This is the result of 20 years of painstaking work carried out by those with the patience of a Persian carpet-weaver.

We try in vain to explain to the Saudis that the only way out of this mess is to unify all anti-Houthi forces under one leadership, controlling all liberated areas and setting all war fronts ablaze at the same time. Instead, the country is being shattered into unrelated armed groups and militias fighting against the legitimate government. It is a mess that I cannot see improving anytime soon.

The Saudis must realise that they are in the same boat as Yemen and much closer to poor Yemenis than to their wealthy Gulf allies. What Iran wants from Yemen and Saudi Arabia is quite different from what it wants from the other Gulf states.

In any case, Iran has already got what it wants from the Gulf states: recognition as the main regional power. Dubai is already the lungs through which it breathes under the suffocating American sanctions. Iran will not stop until both Yemen and Saudi Arabia follow suit.

The international community cares nothing about Yemen and the UN understands nothing about the psychology and the intense desire of the Houthis to rule Yemen, while the UN envoy is either ignorant or just making empty gestures.

Assessing these matters is all part of my daily routine. I try to I communicate my thoughts to my people as best I can. But nowadays these concerns have been amplified by the Covid-19 pandemic, about which I write on social media in the hope of being useful to all my countryfolk, whether they be under Houthi occupation or in liberated parts of the country. But, more than anything, I look forward to the day when my country emerges from this cycle of conflict and calamity and its people can expect a safe, prosperous and fulfilling future.